Coffee County, Tennessee,

Wills, Volume I

1833 – 1860

Originally Prepared By:

The Historical Records Project
Works Progress Administration (WPA)
1936

With New Index

Originally transcribed by:

The Works Progress Administration (WPA)
1936

New Index
Copyright © 1998 by Samuel Sistler

Reprinted by:

Janaway Publishing, Inc.
732 Kelsey Ct.
Santa Maria, California 93454
(805) 925-1038
www.JanawayGenealogy.com

2007, 2012

ISBN: 978-1-59641-062-0

COFFEE COUNTY, TENNESSEE WILLS
VOLUME 1: 1833-1860

transcribed by Mrs. Juanita Overall for the Works
Progress Administration, 1936
with new index by Samuel Sistler, 1998

Please note: This book has two indexes: the first, in the front of the book, is a transcription of the original testator index. The second index, in the back of the book, is a complete index, including slaves noted under their masters' surnames. The index page numbers refer to the original page numbers (along the left edge of the text) and not those of the typed publication itself (in the upper right corner of each page). There are a few instances where both page numbers are given to help the researcher.

We would like to thank Jean Sugg and Chuck Sherrill of the TN State Library and Archives for their kind loan of the original book.

TENNESSEE

RECORDS OF COFFEE COUNTY

WILL BOOK, VOL. 1
1833-1860

HISTORICAL RECORDS PROJECT
OFFICIAL PROJECT NO. 65-44-1439

COPIED UNDER WORKS PROGRESS ADMINISTRATION

MRS. JOHN TROTWOOD MOORE
STATE LIBRARIAN & ARCHIVIST, SPONSOR

ELIZABETH D. COPPEDGE
STATE DIRECTOR OF WOMEN'S & PROFESSIONAL PROJECTS

PENELOPE JOHNSON ALLEN
STATE SUPERVISOR

CAROLINE SMALL KELSO
SUPERVISOR THIRD DISTRICT

COPYIST

MRS. JUANITA OVERALL

APRIL 11, 1936

P-32 In the name of God Amen, I, JOHN CROCKETT of the County of Coffee and State of Tennessee do hereby make and Publish this my last will and testament hereby revoking and making void all other wills by me at any time heretofore made. Item 1st. My will is that all my Just debts be paid by my Executors hereinafter named out of any money I may have on hand or that shall first come into their hands including of course my burial and funeral Expenses. Item 2nd. I give to my daughter Salley Cartwright to her sole and Seperate use free from the debts or control of her husband Eight hundred dollars worth of land with timbers water &c. off of the tract of land on which I now reside the same to be laid off to her by Executors herein after mentioned. Item 3rd. I give to my Grandson William G. Rankins son of my daughter, Nancy Rankins Decd. two hundred dollars in cash to be paid to him by my Executors as soon as may be after my death. Should he die in my lifetime his portion to go to the divises hereinafter named. 4th. Item. The ballance of whatever property real and personal and mixed of which I may die seised and possessed I bequeath to the following children William C. Crocket John T. Crocket Elisa Cunningham Polly Harris & Samuel J Crocket to be equally divided between them share and share alike 5th. I hereby nominate and appoint John T. Crocket and William W. Harris Executor of my last Will and Testament   John Crocket (SEAL)
Signed sealed and witnessed by us in the presence of each other and in the presence of the Testator   Witness
P-33   Uriah Sherrill
                                                   W. B. Hickerson

State of Tennessee
Coffee County
    At a County Court began and held for Coffee County at the Court house in the town of Manchester the 5th day of April 1859 the foregoing last will and testament of John Crockett Deceased was produced to court by the Executors therein named and proven by the oath of William P. Hickerson Uriah Sherrill, the subscribing witnesses thereto and ordered to be recorded which is accordingly done witness my hand at office this 8th. day of April 1859   Hiram S Emerson Clerk

    I, JOHN P. HOWARD of the County of Coffee and State of Tennessee do make and publish this my last will and testament hereby revoking and makeing void all former wills by me at any time heretofore made, And first direct that my body be decently entered at the grave yard on the premises that I now live in said County in a manner suitable to my condition in life and as to such worldly Estate as it has pleased God to intrust me with

I dispose of the same as follows. First: I direct that all my debts be paid as soon after my decease as <u>posible</u> out of any money I may die possessed of or that may come into the hands of my Executors. Secondly: I give and bequeath all my Estate to my beloved wife Sarah Q. Howard both personal and Real during her natural life to dispose among my children equally as she may think fit with the exception of my son William M. Howard, I direct that he shall have two hundred dollars more on account P-34 of him being a cripple. I also direct the portion of property that may fall to my daughter shall be for them and <u>thir</u> bodily heirs forever to be intrusted to them and <u>thir</u> bodily heirs I do hereby make ordain and appointe my beloved wife Sarah Q. Howard Executrix of this my last will and testament In witness whereof I, John P. Howard the said testator have to this my will written on one sheet of paper, set my hand and seal this 31st. day of March in the year of our Lord one thousand Eight hundred and fifty seven   J. P. Howard (SEAL) Sighned, sealed, and published in the presence of the Testator and each other   John P. Hindman
                                          Abner Bryan
                                          J. L. Haynes

State of Tennessee
Coffee County
     At a County Court began and held for Coffee County at the Court house in the town of Manchester on the 4th. day of July 1859, The foregoing last will and Testament of J. P. Howard deceased was produced in Court and proven by the oaths of Abner Bryan and J. L. Haynes subscribing witnesses thereto and ordered to be recorded which is accordingly done this 27th. day of July 1859   Hiram S Emerson Clerk

     Noncupative Will of WILLIAM GILLIAM late of Coffee County Tennessee made in the presence of Thomas P. Stephenson and Jarret Gentry at the house of his Brother A. Gilliam who was sick and where the said William Gilliam had gone to for the purpose of visiting and waiting upon his Brother and while there at his Brothers he was taken sick and died on the 5th day of March P-35 1859 dureing which last sickness he made the following statement about the disposition of his property to wit: He said he wanted his sister Mary Gilliam to have all his property both personal and real after paying his debts, and said that he wanted her to wind up his business for him the same way he would if living, and he wanted her to sue for and collect his debts, the same he would if alive. These statements were made before said Stephenson on the 24th or 25th of <u>Febuery</u> 1859 and before Jarrett Gentry on the 3d day of March 1859 and reduced to writing upon this 14th day of March 1859.

State of Tennessee
Coffee County

This day Thomas P. Stephenson and Jarrett Gentry Personally appeared before me the undersigned Clerk of the County Court of Coffee County in open Court and made oath according to law, that they were present at the tiie and place as mentioned in the foregoing Noncupative Will of William Gilliam and heard him make the statements as above set forth and that they were made dureing his last illness and he had a sound and disposeing mind at the time
Subscribed to and sworn before me on this 4th day of April 1859

Thos. P. Stephenson
Jarrett Gentry
Hiram S. Emerson Clerk

State of Tennessee
Coffee County

This day S. N. Burger Personally appeared before me, the undersigned Clerk of the County Court for said county and made oath according to law that the within noncupative will of William Gilliam was reduced to writing by him on the 14th day of March the time as mentioned in said will by and at the request P-36 of said Thomas P. Stephenson and Harrett Gentry this 4th day of April 1859
Subscribed and sworn to before me on the day and date above written

S. N. Burgher
Hiram S. Emerson Clerk

State of Tennessee
Coffee County

At a County Court began and held for Coffee County at the Court house in the town of Manchester the 4th day of April 1859 The foregoing Noncupative will of William Gilliam deceased was produced to court and proven by the oaths of Phoenus P. Stephenson and Harrett Gentry and ordered to be recorded which is accordingly done witness my hand at office this 11th day of August 1859

Hiram S. Emerson Clerk

In view of the uncertainty of life being feeble in body but sound in mind and anxious while the power is my own so to arrange, settle and dispose of my little temporal effects, with which the gracious Ruler and wise disposer of all events has blessed me so as to prevent any strife coallition or litigation after I am gone the way of all the earth. I do request and will that my body be decently buried yet without pomp or display the expenses of which first to be paid 2d I will and decree that my dearest wife Lavina do receive and hold undisturbed for life and forever at her own disposal the sum in cash of said Estate $3600 as her own personal Estate 3d I will and decree that six hundred Dollars be paid over to the Ten annual P-37 Conference to be disposed as follows. Three hundred dollars to the Ten annual Conf. Missionary society The Interest of which only only ever to be used the other three hundred to be

added to the Preacher aid fund to belong to that society the In
trest of which only to be used. The ballance of said Estate
(save carryall and horses, Books household Furniture Bedding &c
to be my wifes) To be thus disposed of, two hundred dollars to
each of my liveing Brothers and Sisters also two hundred dollars
to the heirs of my brothers George deceased and should there be
a surplus to be proportioned among the above mentioned heirs my
brother Sisters &c. I do hereby authorise and appoint my Dear
beloved wife Levina my Administrator to execute and carry out
this my last will and testament In the name of God, Amen.
Signed by me this 26th Jany. 1852   WM. P. NICHOLS
Witness   Edward Cage
                                         A. D. Cage

State of Tennessee
Coffee County
     At a County Court began and held for Coffee County at the
court house in the town of Manchester on the 6th day of September 1859 the foregoing last will and testament of William P.
Nichols deceased was produced to court by Laviner Nichols the
Executrix therein named and proven by the oath of A. K. Cage one
of the subscribing witnesses thereto, and the other witness Edward Cage being dead the said A. K. Cage State that he was well
acquainted with the handwrighting of the said Edward Cage and
the same was ordered to be recorded which is accordingly done.
Witness my hand at office this 23d day of September 1859
                                   Hiram S. Emerson Clerk

P-38 I,GEORGE D HANCOCK do make and publish this my last will
and testament hereby revoking and making void all other wills
by me at any time made. First I desire that my funeral expenses and all my Just debts be paid as soon after my death as posible out of any moneys I may die possessed of or may first come
into the hands of my Executrix. Secondly, I give and gequeath
to my beloved wife Adelean five thiusand dollars out of my Estate to be hers absolutely and forever I also give her the use
of all my Esteate real and Personal together with all tne rents
and profits thereof during her natural life. Thirdly, should
my said wife hereafter have any natural born child or children,
then it is my desire that all the ballance of my property, Except the five thousand dollars shall go in equal halves to my
own brothers and sisters of my said wife and their heirs, and
lastly, I do hereby nominate and appoint my said wife Adelean
my Executrix. In witness whereof I do to this my last will set
my hand and seal this Oct. 1st day 1859 G. D. Hancock (SEAL)
Signed sealed and published in our presence, and we have subscribed our names hereto in the Presence of the Testator This
Oct. the 1st day 1859   J. A. Brantley
                                      A. Maxwell

P-39 State of Tennessee

Coffee County

At a county Court began and held for Coffee County at the Court house in the town of Manchester on the 2d day of April 1860, The foregoing last will and testament of George D. Hancock, deceased was produced in Court and proven in open Court by the oaths of J. A. Brantley and A. Maxwell the subscribing witnesses thereto and ordered to be recorded which is accouringly done Witness my hand at office this 19th day of April 1860

Hiram S. Emerson Clerk

P-43 I, JACOB KEELE do make and publish this my last will and testament hereby revoking and making void all other wills by me at any time made. First, I direct that my funeral expenses and all my debts be paid as soon as posible out of any moneys I may die Possessed of or that may first come into the hands of my Executors. Secondly, I give and bequeath to my beloved wife Anna dureing her natural life or widowhood all my property of every description of which I may die seised and possessed. Thirdly, I direct that at the death of my said wife all my property except the slaves be sold, the land on a credit of one and two years and the proceeds equally divided amongst my children. Fourthly, I bequeath to my beloved daughter Mary Sparks and the heirs of her body my negro girl Elisa said slave to be valued also I give to my beloved daughter Sarah and the heirs of her body my negro Girl Nancy, said slave also to be valued I further direct that the Ballance of my slaves be valued by disenterested men and divided by lot amongst all my other children except Mary Sparks and Sarah so that in the dividion of my slave property each child shall receive an equal share, and lastly I nominate and appoint John G. Walker my Executor It is my will that if the said slaves Elisa and Nancy or either of them should die before the division of my other slave property that my daughter Mary and Sarah shall have equal shares with the other children of said slaves. In witness whereof I do to this my will P-44 set my hand and seal this the 26th day of Nov. 1852

Jacob (X) Keele (SEAL)

Signed sealed and published in our presence and have subscribed our names hereto in the presence of the testator this Nov. 26th

J. A. Brantley
William Farrar

P-46 I, THOMAS KINDALL of the County of Coffee and State of Tennessee planter do make and publish this my last will and testament hereby revoking and Jaking void all former wills by me at any time heretofore made and first I direct that my body be decently entered in the graveyard at home where I now live in said County In a manner suitable to my condition in life and to each worldly estate as it hath pleased God to Intrust me with I despose of the same as follows. First: I direct that all my Just debts and funeral expenses be paid as soon after my decease as posible out of any moneys I may die possessed of or may first come into the hands of my executors from any portion of my estate real or personal. Secondly, I give and bequeath to my daughter Sarah and the heirs of her body forever to have the forty acres of land including all the houses and buildings where the said Thomas Kindall now lives which is left to my widow dureing her life or widowhood. Thirdly, I give and bequeath to my two sons Waitsdall Avery Coffee Kindall and James Kindall to have the Bal lance of the land divided equally between them and that all three of the children have an equal privelege to fire wood and rail timber on any portion of the place

I do hereby make, ordain and appoint my exteemed neighbors and friend A Maxwell and Wm. Farrar Executors of this my last will and testament, further I do hereby direct that each of them give five dollars a piece to the children of Thomas Kindall de-
P-47 ceased for Whenever they become of age to know how to take care of themselves. I_ witness whereof I Thomas Kindall the testator have to this my last will written on one sheet of paper Set my hand and seal this twenty fourth of May one thousand eight hundred and forty nine   Thomas (X) Kindall
Signed sealed and published in the presence of us the testator and in the presence of each other signed in our presence Sept. the 15th 1851 Test   B. F. Moore
                                         J. A. Brantley

State of Tennessee
Coffee County
At a County Court began and held for Coffee County at the Court house in the town of Manchester of the 7th day of April 1862 The foregoing last will and testament of Thomas Kindall Deceased was produced to Court and proven by the oaths of B. F. Moore and J. A. Brantley the subscribing witnesses thereto and ordered to be recorded which is accordingly done witness my hand at office this 10th day of April 1862   Hiram S. Emerson Clerk

P-48 I, JACOB KEELE do make and publish this my last will and testament hereby revoking and making void all other wills by me at any time made
First. I desire that my funeral expenses and all my debts be paid as soon as possible out of any money I may die possessed of or that may first come into the hands of my executors.
Secondly. I give and bequeath to my beloved wife Anna during her natural life or widowhood all my property of every description of which I may die seised and possessed
Thirdly. I direct that at the death of my said wife all my property except the slaves be sold, the land on a credit of one and two years, and the proceeds equally devided amoung my children
Fourthly. I bequeath to my beloved daughter Mary Sparks and the heirs of her body, my negro girl Eliza, said slave to be valued. Also I give to my beloved daughter Sarah and the heirs of her body, my negro girl Nancy, said slave to be also valued.

I further direct that the balance of my slaves be valued
by disenterested men and divided by lot amoung all my other
children except Mary Sparks and Sarah, so that in the devision
of my slave property each child shall receive an equal share
and lastly I nominate and appoint Jno. G. Walker my executor.
It is my will that the said slaves Eliza and Nancy or either of
them should die before the devision of my other slaves and property, that my doughters Mary and Sarah shall have equal shares
with the other children of said slaves.

In witness whereof I do to this my will set my hand and
seal this 26th day of November 1852   Jacob Keele (SEAL)
p-49 Signed sealed and published in our presence and we have
subscribed our names hereto in the presence of the testator
this Nov. 26th 1852   J. A. Brantley (SEAL)
                                         William Farrar (SEAL)

State of Tennessee
Coffee County

At a County Court began and held for Coffee County at the
Court house in the town of Manchester on the 8th day of October
1861 the foregoing Last will and Testament of Jacob Keele deceased was produced to the Court and proven by the oath of Jas.
A. Brantley one of the subscribing witnesses thereto and ordered to be recorded, which is accordingly Witness my hand at office this 10th day of October 1861   Hiram S. Emerson Clerk

p-84   In the name of God Amen

I Samuel Brown of the County of Coffee and State Tennessee
being now old and frail of body but of sound and desposing mind
and memory do solemnly declare this to be my last will and testament.

1st. It is my will that my daughter Pauline shall inherit
at my death all my personal poiperty of which I may die possessed

2nd. It is my will that my daughter Pauline shall inherit
the lot on which I now live containing two acres bought of Wm.
C. Davis also that she should ingerit the two lots adjoining
said lot one containing half acre and the other containing two
acres bought of the administrator of the estate of Wm. C. Davis
said lots all lying in the town site of Tullahoma in the County
of Coffee

3d. It is my will that my dear wife Susan shall have and
hold at my death two lots adjoining the lots of Benjamin Allen
on the east side of N & C RR in the town of Tullahoma which
lots are now unimproved but are to be improved by me if life
lasts

After my death it is my desire that my daughter Pauline
shall take care of her Mother and that they should live together
but if it should so result that my wife prefers to do so it is
my will that she should have the said lots last mentioned as an
independent home for herself entirely at her disposal

P-85 I hereby bequest Col. P. B. Anderson of the town of Tullahoma to act as the executor of this my last will and testament
and that he be excused from giving security for the execution
of said trust injoined on him by me. In testimony whereof I
have hereunto set my hand and seal this 12th day of July 1854
                                        Samuel (X) Brown (SEAL)
Signed sealed and acknowledged in presence of Test.
                                        E. F. Hunt
                                        C. S. Harris

State of Tennessee
Coffee County
     At a County Court began and held for Coffee County at the
Court house in the town of Manchester on the 7th day of October
1867 the foregoing last will and testament of Samuel Brown de-
deased was produced to Court and proven by the oath of E. F.
Hunt one of the subscribing witnesses thereto and ordered to be
recorded which is accordingly done
          Witness my hand at Office this 12th day of January 1868
                                        Hiram S. Emerson Clerk

     I, NELSON HORTON do this day make and publish this my last
will and testament hereby revoking and making void all other
wills by me at any time made
     1st. I give and bequeath to my beloved wife Perline P. Hor-
ton my tract of land on which I now live and all my stock of every kind together with all my personal property of every description and all debts due to me of every kind for and during
her natural life and at her death or decease the property both
the land and personal property to be devided equally among the
children namely Robert, Nathaniel, Albert, Madison, Collester
Ann Thomas Jeptha Alvira Palestine Charles Grandmon and Harriet
Aminta
P-86-2d, I wish after my decease my executor or administrator
to sell so much of the personal property if it should be neccesd
sary to pay my just debts and funeral expenses and if it should
become neccessary to sell any to sell the property that the family can best spare
     Lastly I nominate and appoint my beloved wife Perline C.
Horton the executrix to this my last will and testament
     In testimony whereof I Nelson Horton have hereunto set my
hand and seal this 12th day of July 1858
                                        Nelson (X) Horton (SEAL)
The above will of Nelson Horton was signed in our presence and
we have here subscribed our names in the presence of the testator at his request this 12th day of July 1858
                                        Silas A. Robinson
                                        Hugh R. Cauthen

State of Tennessee
Coffee County

At a County Court began and held for Coffee County at the Courthouse in the town of Manchester on the 4th day of Feby. 1867 the foregoing last will and testament of Nelson Horton was produced to Court and proven by the oaths of Hugh R Cauthen and Silas A Robinson the subscribing witnesses thereto and ordered to be recorded which is accordingly done this the 12th day of January 1868   Hiram S Emerson Clk.

P-91 State of Tennessee
Coffee County
                    In the name of God Amen
I, LEROY D BEAN being of sound mind and memory and understanding and impressed with the great uncertainty of life and the certain ty of death and being desirous to dispose of my temporal affairs so that after my death no contention may arrise relative to the same
        I Leroy D Bean do make and publish this my last will and testament
        1st. I bequeath my body to the dust whence it came and my soul to God who gave it hoping for happy immortality through the atoning merits of our Lord Jesus Christ the savior of the World
        2nd. That all my Just debts be paid out of my personal and Real Estate by my executrix
        3rd. I give and bequeath to my beloved wife Lucinda Bean (should it please God that she should survive me) all my proper⊥ ty both Real and Personal consisting of my houses and lots in the town of Hillsboro Tennessee with all that pertains thereto together with all my personal property to have and to hold the same for her use and benefit and support during her natural life also any and all Kinds of property both real and personal that I may be possessed of at my death with the right and privilege of selling and desposing of said property either Real or person- al in any manner that she may think proper for her support and benefit
        4th. I desire that after her death that whatever may remain of Real or Personal property should be equally devided between my legal heirs provided they shall apply within twelve months after being notified of her Lucinda Beans death
        Should the application not be made within the time above prescribed by my said heirs, then and in that case I direct and desire that proceeds of said property shall be added to the com mon school fund of the State of Tennessee
        Lastly, I appoint my wife Lucinda Bean my whole and sole executrix to this my will and testament and direct that no se- curity be required for the faithful execution and discharge of the trust hereby reposed in her
        In testimony whereof I have this 3d. day of August 1856 se my hand and seal and in the presence of Leroy D. Bean (SEAL)
                                        B. W. Conn
                                        E. A. Rutherford

P-93 State of Tennessee
Coffee County
    At a County Court began and held for Coffee County at the
Court house in the town of Manchester on the 5th day of July 185
1859 the foregoing last will and testament of Leroy D. Bean deceased was produced to Court by Lucinda Bean the executrix there
in named and proven by the oath of E. H. Rutherford one of the
subscribing witnesses thereto and ordered to be recorded which
is accordingly done
    Witness my hand at office this 10th day of July 1869
                                      Hiram S. Emerson Clk.

P-112 May the 15th One Thousand and Eight Hundred and Thirty-
six,
    Knowing that it is appointed for all men to die and after
this the Judgement, I in my proper senses do will and bequeath
my home tract of land the place whereon I now live between my
two youngest children Richard and Christly Messick equally to
be their land forever, and I do also will and bequeath to my
beloved son Gilbert Messick the tract of land Known be the name
of the Cothern tract of land, to be his property forever and it
is also my wish that Cothern make the deed to my son Gilbert
messick instead of making it to me, And it is also my wish and
my last will and testament that my beloved wife shall have the
land and all the property and shall keep peaceable and undisturbed of the same and all the advantages and benefits of the
place whereon I now live during her lifetime or her widowhood,
and at the death of my wife my wish is that all my property be
sold that is the perishable property and be equally divided between my three beloved daughters Sally Catherine and Polly
    In testimony whereof I set my hand and seal
                                      John Messick (SEAL)
Attest   James W. Wilson
                                      Dabny Ewell
                                      George Messick
                                      Richard Messick
P. S. It is my wish further that my brother Chrisly Messick and
John Frazier act as executors to this my last will and testament
instructions before assigned

P-113   In the name of God Amen
I, WILLIAM QUALLS of the County of Warren and State of Tennessee
taking into consideration the uncertainty of life being now of
sound mind and disposing memory therefore to this I repose and
commend my body to dust from whench it Came and my soul to God
who gave it with hopes of a Joyful resurection through the merits of my Lord and Savior Jesus Christ this 15th day of May in
the year of our Lord 1835
    Item 1st. I give and bequeath unto my son John the whole
tract of land I now live on which contains 77 acres with the
contents thereof and also to my son a bed and furniture and

also my wearing clothes

Item 2nd. I give Martha my wife the all that Marthe my
wife brought with her when we were married

Item 3rd. In general terms I want my Executors or admin-
istrators to put to sale all the rest of my property and after
all my debts are paid then to divide the money equally among
the whole of their heirs to wit: The first heir Martha my wife
Second: Nancy Auston. Third Mary Qualls Forth Elizabeth
Sharp Fifth John Qualls Sixth Louisa Lamb Seventh Sary Gross

Item Last. I do nominate and appoint John Qualls and Clenton Tuder my lawful executors to this my last will and testament
heretofore by me made in testimony whereof I have hereunto set
my hand and affixed my seal this 13th day of May (1835) one
Thousand Eight Hundred and Thirty five William (X) Qualls
Attest   Kinchan Martin
                                          David Conlston

P-114   In the Name of God Amen
    I, JOSEPH TAYOLR of Franklin County and State of Tennessee
being sick but of sound mind and memory (thanks be given to God)
Calling to mind the mortality of my body and Knowing that it is
appointed unto all men to die do make and ordain this my last
will and testament, that is to say

    1st of all I wish my wife Rebecca to live on the one hun-
dred and fifty acre tract where I now live, to raise the children and to keep the big sorrell mare and all of my stock of cattle and hogs and ten head of sheep for the support of the family
and all the household furniture and working utensils

    And if my wife should marry I want the land sold and equal-
ly devided betwaen her and my children and also Give unto my son
Drury the Colt he claims also give my gun to my son James the
property that is sold after my debts are paid I want the profit
to be put to the schooling of my children Ratifying and Confirming this my last will and testament. In witness whereof I have
hereunto set my hand and seal this 24th day of May 1833
                                 Joseph (X) Taylor (SEAL)
Signed Sealed and delivered by the said Joseph Taylor as his
last Will and Testament in presence of us
                                 Abm. Veny Vendall
                                 William Collins
                                 Harden Taylor

P-115   In the name of God Amen
    I, WILLIAM DANIEL SR. of the County of Coffee and State of
Tennessee being weak in body but of sound and perfect mind and
memory blessed be Almighty God for the same do make and publish
this my Last Will and Testament in manner and form following
that is to say,

    1st. I give and bequeath to my beloved wife Elizabeth
Daniel the two hundred acre tract of land on which I now live,

all the two hundred acre tract of land on which I now live, all
the household and Kitchen furniture and working tools, and the
horses hogs, cattle, sheep and every other article onf the
place also these slaves (to wit) Charles, Dinah and her natural
increase and Sarah during her natural life or widowhood and at
her death the above named property is to be equally divided a-
mong her eight children to wit James, John, Morgue Thomas Polly Eliza Ann. Mott and Stark my large gun I wish to be sold and
the price of it to be appropriated to the schooling of my two
youngest sons Wiatt and Stark I then direct that my land on
Riley's Creek and my negro man John to be sold and the money
which they bring be divided among my first wifes children as
follows To my beloved son Walter Daniel I give and bequeath
one dollar in cash and the remainder to be equally divided a-
mong the other six children viz. Eilliam Daniel Sarah Wall Sam-
ual Daniel Elizabeth Y daniel Henrietta Clancy and John Daniel
this being all that I am able to give them at this time, After
paying all my just debts I give and bequeath unto my beloved
Elizabeth Daniel all the bonds notes and monies which will be l
left all my personal estate not otherwise named I bequeath unto my said wife Elizabeth Daniel whom I appoint Executrix and
P-116 her son James Daniel Executor of this my last Will and
Testament hereby revoking all former wills by me made I_ witness whereof I have hereunto set my hand and seal this Twenty S
seventh day of February in the year of our Lord one thousand
Eight hundred and Thirty six   William (X) Daniel
                                                    (SEAL)

Signed sealed in our presence   S. Murray
                                       Wm. Wright
                                       S. McClain

       The last Will and Testament of the testator SANFORD BERRY
of Coffee County and State of Tennessee this 25th day of August
in the year of our Lord 1836 in which I commend my spirit to
God that gave it and my body to the earth from whence it came
       Item 1st. I first desire that my just debts be paid
       Item 2nd. I will to my daughter Annie Kelton have and e-
qual share with my legatees
       Item 3rd. I will that my son William Berry have an equal
share with my legatees with the exception of two hundred dollars which he received in a negro man Minga

Item 4th. I will that my daughter, Sarah Hunter have and equal share with my legatees with the exception of fifty dollars which she received in cash

Item 5th. I will that my daughter Christina Davis have an equal share with my legatees

Item 6th. I will that my son Edward Berry have an equal P-117 share with my legatees after the deduction of one hundred dollars which he received in a copper still

Item 7th. I will that my son Samuel Berry have an equal share with my legatees

Item 8th. I will that my son John Berry have and equal share with my legatees

Item 9th. I will that my daughter Namin Frazier have an equal share with my legatees with the exception of three hundred dollars for which she received a negro woman

Item 10th. I will that my daughter Margaret Carden have an equal share with my legatees

Item 11th. I will that my son Josiah Berry have an equal share with my legatees

Item 12th. I will that my daughter Elizabeth Jones have no divide with my legatees she having received to the amount of Eight hundred dollars in Negro property Givne also by deed of Gift,

And I hereby nominate instruct and appoint my sons John and Josiah my executor to this my last will and testament to dispose of my personal property and lands by public sale or otherwise as may be thought expedient In witness whereof I have hereunto set my hand and affixed my seal, the day and date first above written Sealed and signed in the presence of   Sanford (X) Berry(SEAL)
Attest   Thomas Mitchell
                                             Jobe Mitchell

                    In the name of God Amen
The sixth day of November one thousand eight hundred and thirty P-118 seven I, WILLIAM MARSHALL in the County of Coffee and State of Tennessee of sound mind and memory but weak in body do make this my last Will and Testament at the same time revoking all former wills verbal or otherwise

1st. It is my will and wish that all my Just debts shall be paid

2nd. I give and bequeath to my beloved wife Margarett Marshall all my lands stock furniture &C. real and personal to have and to hold during her material lifetime.

3rd. At her decease it is my will that the land which is three hundred acres be equally divided between my sons whose names are these John Mayhall William Mayhall Henry Mayhall and Berry Mayhall which are my sons and James B. Mayhall who is my Grandson to hold the horse which he now has and have equal shares of the land.

4th. It is my will and wish that the balance of the property be equally divided between my daughters whose names are these

Elizabeth Farmer Katie Allen Sarah Walker Feyy Mayhall and
Nany Mayhall, then at the decease of Margaret Mayhall shall
the above named heirs be duly entitled to another estate so bequeathed to them by their father, land stock and furniture and
everything I possess either real or personal to be divided as
the above directs

I do appoint my beloved wife my executrix to carry out
this instrument into effect In witness whereof I have here into
set my hand and seal this day and state above written
                    William (X) Mayhall (SEAL)
Signed sealed and delivered in prisence of us Daniel McLean
                    John Armstrong

p-119 I, WILLIAM ROBERTSON of the County of Coffee and State of
Tennessee planter do make and publish this my last Will and Test
ament hereby revoking and making void all former wills by me at
any time heretofore made

1st. I direct that my body be decently entered in a manner
suitable to my condition in life and to such worldly estate as it
has pleased God to intrust me with I dispose of the same as follows

1st. I direct that all my debts and funeral expenses be paid
as soon after my decease as possible.

2nd. I give and bequeath unto my son William Robertson and
my daughter Elizabeth and Nancy (which three children one by my
first wife) one cow and calf each and to my daughter Eliza I
give one bed and furniture and one cow and calf. All of the rest
of my children by my first wife I have heretofore given them the
portion that I allow them and lastly I give and bequeath to my
beloved wife Telitha all the residue of my estate both real and
personal to be possessed of & by her to be made use of for her
own and her childrens benefit that she has had by me, as she
may think proper for raising and schooling said children In wit
ness whereof I have set my hand this 7th day of October 1838
                    Wm. (X) Robertson (SEAL)
Signed sealed and published in presence of us who have subscribed
in the presence of the testator and in presence of each other
Attest   Benjamin F. Jenkins
                               William Robertson
                               Sibby Shed

P-120 I, JANE CAUTHRAN of the County of Coffee and State of Tennessee do make and publish this my last Will and Testament revoking and making void all former wills by me at any time heretofore
made and first I desire that my body be decently entered at the
grave yard near a meeting house called Wells Meetinghouse in Cannon County Tennessee in a manner suitable to my condition in life
and as to what worldly estate it has pleased God to intrust me
with I wish disposed of in the following manner

1st. I direct that all my Just debts be paid as soon after
my death as convenient out of any moneys that I may die possessed

of or that may first come into the hands of my executors from any portion of my estate real or personal

2nd. It is my desire that all my property both real and personal except my wearing clothes be sold on a twelve months credit and the proceeds thereof to be equally divided among my eight children to wit: Elizabeth Thompwon Ebi Hill William R Corthren Martin Couthran Pleasant Cauthran Milly Whiteman Mathilde McCulliugh and Felisha Laird and that my wearing Clothes be equally devided among my four daughters above named.

3rd. I do hereby make ordain and appoint my esteemed neighbor and friend Daniel Dabny East Executor of this my will and testament in witness whereof I Jane Couthron the said testator hath to this my last will written on one peace of paper set my hand and seal this twenty fifth day of August one thousand eight hundred and thirty eight. The

P-121

Jane (X) Couthron   (SEAL)
John F. Morrison
John B. Wiser
James H. Roughton

I, THOMAS KING being of sound and perfect mind and memory do make and publish this my last Will And Testament in the manner and form following.

1st. I will that out of the proceeds of my crop and such property as wife thinds con be best spared all my Just debts and funeral expenses be paid by my executors

2nd. After the payments of my debts I give and bequeath to my beloved wife Elizabeth King all my real and personal property of what kind and nature so ever during her natural life excepts such parts and portion thereof as may be hereinafter by me devised. 3rd. I give to my son Richard S King an interest with his mother in the plantation on which I now reside in order that he may manage to take care of the same for his motner and for his own support not allowing him to use the profits of the said plantation for extravagant or profligate purposes.

4th. I give and bequeath to my doughter Hannah Parten a negro girl Ann about eight months old which she has in her possession for her own seperate use and benefit and not for the use benefit or control of her said husband during my said daughters natural life and at her death the said negro girl and her increas to be divided among the children of my said daughter Hannah Parten

5th.To each of my sons John and Richard I gave a cow and calf Bed and furniture &C. to be for them selected out of my estate by my wife so as to make them equal in this respect with my other children who have gone to housekeeping. I also give to my son Richard S. a young black forse saddle and bridle which are now called his

P-122

6th. I will that all my estate Real and Personal of what kind and nature soever remaining at the death of my wife Elizabeth King shall be equally divided among my children Charles King Wil-

liam King Jessy King Richard S King Hannah Parten and Mary Nevill and Elizabeth Burrows or their lawful heirs
    7th. Lastly I hereby nominate and appoint William S. Mooney
and Beverly Burrows executors of this my last will and testament
hereby revoking all former wills by me made. In witness whereof
I have hereunto set my hand and seal this Eighth day of Jone
Eighteen hundred and thirty six signed sealed and published by
the above named Thos King sr. to be his last will and testament
in the presence of us who have hereunto subscribed our names as
witnesses in the presence of the testator W. S. Mooney
                    Walter Mileham
                Thomas (X) King(SEAL)
Proven by W. S. Mooney at the July Term 1840 as appears of Record
                Hiram S. Emerson

I, JAMES YELL do make and publish this my last will and testament
hereby revoking and making void all other wills by me at any
time made
    1st. I desire that my funeral expenses and all my debts be
P-123 paid as soon after my death as possible out of any money
that I may die possessed of or that may first come into the hand
of my executors
    2nd. I give and bequeath to my well beloved wife Jenitia
Yell my plantation and houses during her natural lifetime or
widowhood to enable her to raise and educate my children
    3rd. My daughter Cintha Held as was I do not want her heirs
to have any part of my estate as I gave her in her lifetime as
much in land horses bed &C. as would come to her part
    4th. I give and bequeath to my son Francis M Yell the fol-
lowing tract of land to wit: Beginning at a branch comes running west across a lake or bio to the foot of a bluff, thence
southwardly with the meanders of the foot or the bottom of the
hill or bluff up the river eastwardly to where a creek or branch
comes in thence up said hollow south opposite a beginning corner of a tract I bought of Gray W. Haggard and the said Haggard
bought of Felix Campbell, thence with the lines of said tract
eastwardly to the southwest corner of a tract formerly the property of Isham Evants thence northwest with my line to the River,
thence with the meanderings of the south banks of said river
down to the beginning
    5th. I give and bequeath to my other children to wit: Jane
Yell, Lucy Yell, Benjamin Yell, Joshua Yell, Dorah Yell and Ruth
S. Yell, When my youngest comes of age I wish all my lands here
tofore unbequeathed to be sold and the proceeds to be equally
devided between them and my wife Jenitia
P-124 Lastly I hereby appoint and nominate my wife Janitha Yell
and my son Francis M. Yell my executors:
    In witness whereof I do to this my last will and testament
set my hand and seal this fourth day of November 1839
                James Yell (SEAL)
Signed sealed and published in our presence and we have sub-

scribed our names hereto in the presence of the testator this
4th. day of November 1839   John Compbell
                                             Felix Campbell

State of Tennessee
Coffee County
     In the name of God Amen , I, THOMAS HARRISON now being in
perfect health and mind and memory do make and publish this my
last will and testament
     1st. I want to be buried decently and all my funeral ex-
penses to be paid out of my estate then I loan to my beloved
wife Nancy Harrison the plantation on which I now live and of my
negroes and their further increase to wit: Nannie and Diley
and Caroline and James and Isaac and Mary and all of my horses
of every description and all my hogs sheep and cattle of every
description and all my stock of any kind whatsoever Kind it may
be and all of my household and Kitchen furniture and I give and
bequeath all and every specia of property as above named to my
beloved wife Nancy Harrison during her natural lifetime then at
her death all of my estate to be equally divided among my seven
children (to wit) William Harrison Elizabeth McCrary, Jusomah
Sartin and Thomas Harrison and Elizah Harrison and Johnson Harrison and Aaron Harrison to my executors to be my executors this
my last will and testament
     Given under my hand and seal this 11th. day of September
1838   Thomas (X) Harrison (SEAL)
Signed sealed and delivered in presence of us
                                 James Mayo
                                 Bazel Timmons

     I, JOHN CATE do make and publish this my last will and test
ament hereby revoking and making void all other wills by me at
any time made
     1st. I direct that my funeral expenses and all my debts be
paid as soon after my death as possible out of any monies that
I may die possessed of or that may first come into the hands of
my executors
     2nd. I give and bequeath to my beloved wife Priscilla Cate
one Black mare cow and calf, My entire stock of sheep and hogs,
one bed and furnitures and all my kitchen furniture.
     3rd. I give to the lawful heirs of my daughter Polly the
following property (which my said daughter Polly received in her
lifetime) Viz. one bed and furniture and one side saddle
     4th. I give to my daughter Susanna one bed and furniture
which she has in her possession and one heiffer
     5th. I give to my daughter Sarah Harriet one bed and furn-
iture and cow and calf
P-126 6th. I give to my daughter Biddy one bed and furniture and
one cow and calf which property she has in her possession
     7th. I give to my son John B. Cate one mare and bed and
furniture and one cow and calf which he has in his possession

8th. I give to my son Elizah Cate one horse and bed and furniture and one cow and calf all of which he has heretofore received

9th. I give to my son Henry A. Cate one gray mare one bed and furniture and one cow and calf

10th. I give to my three sons John B. Elizah and Henry A my wagon to be equally amoung them

11th. I direct that my executor shall sell all my property that has not heretofore been disposed of by this will and after making such disposition of the proceeds as are provided for in the first section of this my last will and testament, divide the remainder equally among my four daughters herein before named and the heirs of their body.

Lastly, I do hereby nominate and appoint Alexander E. Patton my executor.

In witness whereof I do to this will set my hand and seal this 22d. day of April 1840   John Cate   (SEAL)
Signed Sealed and published in our presence and we have subscribed our names hereto in the presence of the testator this 22d. day of April 1840   John Lefever
                                                     B. C. Stonestreet

P-127   In the name of God Amen
I, DAVID COALSON of the County of Warren and State of Tennessee Planter taking into consideration the uncertainty of life and being of sound mind and memory do constitute, make and publish this my last will and testament

In primus I command my body to the dust from whence it came and my soul to God who gave it, with hopes of a Joyful resurrection through the merits of our Lord and Savior Jesus Chr Christ

Item 1st. I give and bequeath unto my beloved brothers Henry, John and James Conlson five dollars each I give and bequeath to my beloved sisters Rachael Belliums Fanny Hastings and Mary Wallace five dollars each

Item 3rd. I give devise and bequeath to my wife Sarah Conlson and to each all of my children on the rest and resicue of my estate both Real and Personal to be divided to them by my executors as they come of age

It is also my wish that my wife do not have the sole right to her share so delivered her until the youngest child may have come of age, but to continue together until that period, and over and above the equal share given to my beloved wife it is my sill and wish that she shall have choice of a Negro man and woman in addition for and during her natural life, and at her death the whole and every part of her share of my estate so bequeathed to her to be equally destributed and divided between the whole of my children,

In relation to the sale of my surplus stock and to the management of all the rest of my affairs that I do not specially mention I love to be done in that way which my executor

may deem most expedient and proper for the interest of my said
heirs

P-128 And lastly I do hereby constitute ordain and appoint my
two sons Charles and James Conlson of the County of Warren and
State of Tennessee my lawful executors to this my last will and
testament hereby revoking all former wills and testaments heretofore by me made

In testimony whereof I have hereunto set my hand and seal
this the 21st of February in the year of our Lord one thousand
eight hundred and thirty three   David C. (X) Conlson(SEAL)
Signed sealed and delivered in the presence of us

Thomas Woodfin
Clinton Tinker
Kinchen Mathews

JAMES OAKS' WILL

I, JAMES OAKS of the County of Coffee and State of Tennessee do
make and publish this my last will and testament hereby revoking
and making void all former wills heretofore made by me

1st. I direct that my body be decently intered in said
county in a manner suitable to my condition in life

As to such worldly estate as it has pleased God to intrust
me with I dispose of the same as follows

1st. I direct that my debts and funeral expenses be paid
as soon as possible after my decease with the first monies that
come into the hands of my executors

2nd. I do give and bequeath to my beloved wife two horses
two cows and calves, a yoke of oxen and cash and what few hogs
I have to be her right and property to help raise my children

3rd. I bequeath to my beloved wife the plantation Known by
P-129 the Douglass place to reside and raise the children on
for fifteen years after which time It may be sold and divided
among my lawful heirs

I divise that the Harp place be sold so soon as it can be
done for cash but if there should not come money enough into
the hands of my executors after collecting my debts and selling
all the stock except what I have given to my wife, then and in
that case I want the Harp place sold to the best advantage and
theproceeds applied to paying of the debts and if it should not
be sold, I want it rented out and it sold or divided among my
heirs when the other land is

4th. I desire for the black woman Lucretia to be hired out
after the expiration of the present year and the yellow boy Jim
as soon as he is large enough both to be hired out yearly until
the land is sold or divided among my heirs and I want my beloved wife to keep the other little girl named Rose until the devision of the land to help raise the children and then all the
negroes and their increase and the proceeds of the hire and the
proceeds arising from the sale or rent of the Harp place if
there should be any and equally devided among my heirs

I do hereby appoint ordain and make my esteemed friend and

neighbors Obedial Freeman and my beloved son Isaac Executors of
this my last will and testament

In witness whereof I James Oaks the said testator have to
this my will set my hand and seal this the 7th day of January
in the year of our Lord one thousand eight hundred and forty one

James Oaks (SEAL)

Signed sealed and published in the presence of us who have subscribed in the presence of the testator and each other

Thomas A. Brown
Henry Hamaker

P-130   WILLIAM SHEDS WILL
State of Tennessee
Coffee County

Know all men by these presents that WILLIAM SHED SR. of
the County and State aforesaid for and and in consideration of
the good feelings and love and affections I have for my daughter Anna Harris and John Harris my son in law and also for Care
and Kindness done towards me the said William Shead hereunto
have given granted & confirmed and do by these presents give
grant and confine unto the said Anna and John Harris all and
singalar the following articles (viz) One feather bed and furniture with some house hold and kitchen utensils to tedious to
mention. Also one boy and also one half of the proceeds of
four hundred acres of land after fifteen dollars are deducted
our of the said land lying and being in the State of South Car-
olina, Pickens District, When sold by my agent Edward Huse, the
other half of the proceeds of said land for my son James Shed
and alson one feather bed and furniture for said James Shed the
same to the only proper use and benefit and behalf of said John
and Anna Harris and James and George Shed their heirs and as-
signs forever and I the said William Shed Conclude.

Given under my hand and seal this 8th day of September
1840   William Shed (SEAL)
Attest   Isham Womack
                               A. L. I. Womack

P131 The last Will and Testament of Joseph Carney deceased.

I, JOSEPH CARNEY of the County of Coffee and State of
Tennessee being sound in mind but weak in body and wishing to
arrange all my earthly business, do make and publish this my
last will and testament hereby revoking and making void all
other wills by me at any time made

1st. I direct that my funeral expenses and all my debts be
paid as soon after my death as possible out of any money that
I may die possessed of or that may first come into the hands of
my executors

2nd. I give and bequeath unto my beloved wife Mary Carney
all my household and kitchen furniture to act with and dispose
of as she may think proper

I give unto my beloved wife Mary all that portion of the

Land belonging to the tract I now live on, on the side of the Garrison Fork of Duck River on which are my dwellings and south of the road leading to Manchester, during her lifetime

I also give unto my beloved wife Mary during her lifetime all of my farming tools and utensils my cart and two oxen also two other steers and five milk cows and calves. I give my wife Mary all my hogs and sheep now in my possession and the choice of two of my horses.

I do also give unto my beloved wife Mary during her lifetime the following negroes viz. Hector, Monday, Indy, Judy, Pat zy and child of Pegys during her natural life.

3rd. I give unto my daughter Noahmah all the balance of my stock not above mentioned horses and cattle, and I give unto my P-132 daughter Noahmah my Negro Woman Patty and her child and negroe girl Edy and Boys Tony and Davy

The negroe woman Patey and her child however to remain as first stated with my beloved wife during her lifetime

4th. I give and bequeath my grandson Signard H. Carney all my land situated on the south and East side of Garrison fork of Duck River at the death of my wife Mary, and I also will that my Grandson Legrand H. Carney take into possession at my death all that portion of the above mentioned land lying east of the road leading through it to Manchester

I also will and bequeath unto my grandson Legrand H. Carney the following negroes viz: Mondy and George the negro Mon day however as first to remain with my wife Mary during her natural life and then to be my Grandson Legrand H. Carneys. I also wish that my negro man Tom be sold and four hundred dollar of his price be given to Isabelle Taylor if she lives to be ten years old and when she arrives at that age, and the balance of the price of Tom I will and bequeath to my grandson Legrand H. Carney I however make this provision, that if Legrand H. Carney prefer Keéping Tom and paying the four hundred dollars that he shall do so. It is my wish and will that Tom shall have a selection of his master if sold.

5th. I will and bequeath unto my Grandson Smith Carney at the death of my beloved wife Mary the following negroes viz. Hector and Judy. I also will and bequeath unto my Grandson Sanders B Carner my negro man Peter and all my black-smith tool It is also my wish that my Grandson L. A. Carney should see P-133 proper to farm on that portion of land above mentioned that my negro woman Cherry and Nannie Shall remain thereon, not subjects not as slaves to him but their labor to be for their own benefit but in case he should keep any hands here it is my wish that Cherry shall be placed under the care & charge of Grandson Smith Carney and that Nannie be placed under care and charge of my Grandson Sanders R Carney neither of them do I wish to be considered as servants or Slaves in any wise but that they be permitted to use their own labor for their support.

I will and bequeath unto my Granddaughter Susan Sparks my negro woman Clarissa provided she is willing to go to her, but

if not it is my wish that she shall be sold in the neighborhood
of her husband belonging to Wilson Norton and that the prefer-
ence be given to said Norton to purchase her upon said terms for
cash or part cash and the balance on time and the proceeds to be
given to my granddaughter Susan, above mentioned.

All of this I do fully willand bequeath to the different i
individuals as above stated

I also so wish and desire that my three Srandsons viz. Sanders H. Carney, Smith Carney and Legrand H Carney act as my executors

I_ witness whereof I hereunto set my hand and seal this 22-
d day of February in the year of our Lord Eighteen hundred and
forty one   Joseph (X) Carney   (SEAL)
Signed and sealed in presence of us   William Sharp
                                       Alexander Downing
                                       James Frizzel

                           Codicil
         To the last will and testament of Joseph Carney
         Item 1st. It is my will and desire that my Grandson P. Har-
rison should have at my death my negro boy Josh
         Item 2nd. I have given to my grandson Smith Carney all my
P-134 lands on the North and west side of Duck River which are
described by meets and bounds in a deed made by me to him and
now in my possession which deed I desire may be delivered to
him at my death,
         Item 3d. I hereby appoint my Grandson Legrand H Carney
guardian for Issabella Taylor and I desire that he should take
Care of the four hundred willed to her and pay the same over to
her at her marriage or arrival at eighteen years of Age. I do
not intend hereby that in case of her death before the money is
paid over to her the above shall go to him, the same shall go
to his heirs on the contrary I desire the same to be devided in
that event between my heirs. It is my wish that the interest
upon the four hundred dollars above mentioned be applied as it
is convenient to the education of my said Granddaughter Issabella
         It is my desire that my Grandson Smith Carney and Legrand
H. Carney act as my executors hereby revoking that part of the
will appointing the executors.
         I hereby direct that all my money and effects not herein
or in my will bequeather or devided be devided equally among my
heirs March 14th 1841   Joseph (X) Carney (SEAL)
Attest   H. Yoakum
                                     A. Mitchell

         The Noncupative will of JOHN LEFEVER DECD.
         We John Wilson W. B. Willis Hirom Smith and E. A. Patton
do state that the Noncupative will of John Lefevers was made by
him on the 26th day of May 1841, in our presence by the testator
 himself in the presence of each other that was made in his last

P-135 sickness (caused by a wound) in the dwelling house of
Samuel Lowe, and the same is as follows to wit: (He Lafevers
called his wife to him and said) Old woman I am going to die.
I wish you to have me a plain coffin made and bury me under
that big apple tree in the garden. You take out as much of the
property as you want and make a sale and sell the balance, pay
all my just debts and I want every man to have his rights you ke
keep the balance and live on it you will have a plenty if you
will live saving. I bought Burns land for two hundred and fifty one dollars you unst have a deed for it

I have a good deal of money owing to me get it if you can
and if you cannot you can live without it. Made out by us and
signed this 2nd day of June 1841   John Wilson (SEAL)
                                        William B. Willis(SEAL)
                                        Hirom (X) Smith (SEAL)
                                        A. E. Patton (SEAL)

                In the name of God Amen

I, DUNCAN NEILE of the County of Coffee and State of Tennessee being weak in body but of sound and perfect mind and memory considering the uncertainty of this mortal life and being
of sound &C. Blessed be Almighty God for the same do make and
publish this my last will and testament in manner and form following that is to say:

Item 2nd. I give and bequeath unto my beloved wife Betty
the sum of One hundred and fifty dollars with bed and bedding.

Item 1st. I give and bequeath to my Soul to God who gave
it.

Item 3rd. I do give and bequeath unto my son James Neil
the plantation where I now live on with all of my lands on the
South side of Duck River running up to John Carrolls Spring
branch

Item 4. I also will and bequeath to my beloved wife Bettie
P-136 her life estate on the land while she remains my widow or
she sees cause to stay on the land to my two youngest James
Neile and Angelina Neil and they are to be educated on the profits arising therefrom.

Item 5th. I also will and bequeath unto Elizabeth Neil her
life estate on the land where I now live with wood and water &
land for any cultivation she sees proper so long as she remains
single and sees proper to live on the land, then and in that
case then her claim or claims to cease on said land and all of
my movable property to be sold and the proceeds to be devided a-
mong the following heirs excepting my servant John who shall not
be sold under six years after my death but shall remain as a
slave on the plantation for the benefit of the family who resides here and then to be sold and to be disposed of as the balance of the property

Item 6th. I also do make Elizabeth Neil my lawful heir to
her part of the property that is to be sold likewise Thomas Neil
Eliza Campbell Alexander Neil Mary Oldfield, Nancy Oldfield as
for William Neil and James Neil they have received their part

excepting five dollars each.

I do hereby appoint my son Alexander Neil Administrator of this my last will and testament hereby revoking all former wills by me made:

In witness whereof I have hereunto set my hand and affixed my seal the 20th day of November eighteen hundred and forty.

Duncan Neil (SEAL)

Signed sealed published and delivered by the above named Duncan Neil to be his last will and testament in the presence of us who have hereunto subscribed our names as witnesses in the presence of the testator. Attest 　　　　　John Penn
　　　　　　　　　　　　　　　　　　　　　　Daniel Hardaway

Will of HUGH DAVIDSON Deceased

In the name of God Amen, I, HUGH DAVIDSON of Coffee County and State of Tennessee, being in good health and sound in body and mind and Desposing memory for which I thank God and calling to mind the uncertainty of human life and being desirous to despose of all my worldly substance as it has pleased God to bless me with I give and bequeath in the manner following that is to say.

1st. I give and bequeath ot my beloved wife Jane my tract of land for her use and benefit during her natural lifetime although I leave descriptionary with my executors to sell said land for the benefit and use of my beloved wife Jane her natural lifetime.

I also give and bequeath to my beloved wife Jane the following perishable property to wit.

My negroe man Ben, my negroe man Lambert my negroe woman Hannah my negroe girl Ann my negroe girl Mary also my negroe man Andy also all my stock of every description together with all my house hold and kitchen furniture and all my farming tol tools to her use and benefit her material lifetime with the desintionary power to sell and surplus property and dispose of the proceeds there of to the most needy of my lawful heirs P-138 2d. I give and bequeath to my son William M Davidson the following property to wit:

Two hundred acred of land in the western district which he has already gotton worth four hundred dollars, I also bequeath to same four hundred which he has aready got.

3rd. I also give and bequeath to my doughter Pricilla Britton one negro girl named Ibby worth three hundred dollars which she has already gotton

4th. I also beuqeath to my daughter Margaret Guinn one negroe girl worth four hundred.

5th. I give and bequeath to my son David W. Davidson one negroe boy named Gradison worth three hundred dollars which he has got.

6th. I also give and bequeath to my daughter Angelina Morgan one negro girl Mary worth three hundred and fifty dollars which she has got and had in her possession and disposed of.

7th. I also give and bequeath to my son John Davidson one negroe man named named Kit worth seven hundred dollars which he has already got, I also give and bequeath to the same three hundred dollars which he has already gotton

8th. I also give and bequeath to my son Samuel L. Davidson one negroe man Isaac worth seven hundred dollars which he has got I also give the same three hundred dollars which he has got ton

9th. I give and bequeath to my son Hugh Davidson one negro boy Alfred with five hundred Dollars which he has already got and eight hundred dollars which he has got for expenditures in receiving his education.

10th. I give and bequeath to my son Robt. B. Davidson my negroe boy Henderson worth three hundred dollars to the same I give two hundred dollars which he has already got

P-139 11th. I also give and bequeath to my daughter Marthy ann Davidson my negrow girl Caroline worth five hundred dollars I also five to the same one horse beast worth eighty and such other consideration as my elder daughters have received when they went to housekeeping

It is my will that all my heirs at law should be made e- qual at the winding up of my estate

Lastly I also appoint my beloved wife Jane Davidson Exe- cutrix and my son Samuel L Davidson and my son Hugh L. David- son my executors of this my last will and testament in witness whereof I hereunto set my hand and seal this 7th day of July 1839

(on the back of the will)   Hugh L. Davidson(SEAL)

My will and desire is that Priscella Britton have one hundred and fifty dollars ehich she has received also to my son Samuel Davidson I give and bequeath one hundred dollars this 14th September 1841   Hugh Davidson (SEAL)
Attest   Samuel Vance
                                             A. M. Holt

                  MORTON JONES WILL
                In the name of God Amen
I,MORTON JONES of the County of Coffee and State of Tennessee being in proper health and mind thanks be to God Calling unto mind the mortality of my body and knowing that it appoint to all men once to die, do make and ordain this my last will and testament that is to say principally and before all I give and recommend my soul into the hands of Almighty God that give it, and my body I recommend to the earth to be buried in a decent christian like manner at the direction of my executors and as touching such worldly estate as it has pleased God to help me inthis life I dispose of in the following manner
P-140 1st. I give and bequeath to Nancy Jane my dearly beloved wife all my property to wit: My negroe boy Sammy, Stock of horses hogs cattle and house hold and kitchen furniture and farming utensils during her natural lifetime and at her death

my will is that my executors sell all my estate on a credit of
twelve months and the money arising from the sale of my said
property to be equally devided among my children in the following manner to wit.

I will to my son Hugh Jones one bed and furniture my saddle and briddle over and above his equal share with the rest of
my heirs. My will is that the lawful heirs of Gabriel Jones receive two dollars each and no more.

I will to my son Joseph D Jones two dollars and no more
and the balance to be devided equally between Morton Jones,
Francis Foster, Benjamin Jones.

I likewise constitute and appoint make and ordain Eli Petty
and Hugh Jones the sole executors to this my last will and testament hereby revoking and making void all former wills by me at
any time made.

Ratifying and confirming this and no other to be my last
will and testament

In witness whereof I have hereto set my hand and seal this
Thirtieth day of May in the year of our Lord one thousand eight
hundred and forty   Morton (X) Jones (SEAL)
Signed Sealed and published in presence of us,
                                                 Henry Powers
                                                 Mitchell Stephens

GEORGE D SHERRILL'S WILL
In the name of God Amen---
I GEORGE D SHERRILL of the County of Coffee and State of Tennessee being weak in body but of sound mind and memory thanks to
Almighty God for his mercies, calling to mind the mortality of
my body and knowing that it is appointed unto all men once to
die do make and ordain this my last will and testament that is
to say

1st. I give and bequeath unto my five Children that are yet
living with me to wit Nancy Sherrill Penina Sherrill Dascas G
Sherrill FES. Sherrill and Mary B Sherrill the following tracts
of land to wit,

One tract of three hundred and fifty acres entered in the
entry takers office of Franklin County on the 7th day of May
eighteen hundred and twenty seven grant no 546 and registered
in the registers office of the mountain district in Book A page
412. Also one other tract of land containing 400 acres entered
in the entry takers office of Franklin County on the sixth day
of January eighteen hundred and twenty six grant no 547 Registered in the registers office of the mountain District in Book
A page 413. One other tract of land containing one hundred
acres entered in the entry takers office of Franklin County on
the 31st day of March 1826 grant no 714 Recorded in the registers office of the mountain District in Book B, page 146, one
other tract of land containing one hundred acres and entered
in the entry takers office of Franklin County the 3d day of
July 1824 grant no. 5626 Recorded in the Registers office of

west Tennessee in Book No. F. One tract of land containing ten acres it being part of certificate no. 2198, dated 26th day of September 1815 Entered on the 30th day of March 1822 by no 1208 Grant No. 20890 Recorded in registers office of West Tennessee the 12th day of February 1824, One other tract containing forty acres and being part of Certificate No. 2198 and dated 26th September 1815 entered on the 30th of March 1822 Grant No 20891 Recorded in Registers office of West Tennessee 12th Feby 1824 p-142 One other tract of land Containing sixteen acres being part of Certificate no 2182 dated the 25th day of September 1815 entered on the first day of June 1822 by no 12100 Recorded in the Registers office of West Tennessee 12th day of February 1824 in all one thousand and sixteen hundred acres to be equally devided among my said five children to wit Nancy, Penina Darcas G. IT Sherril and Mary B according to its value

I further give and bequeath unto my four daughters that live with me to wit: Nancy Penina Darcas G. and Mary B. all my stock of horses cattle hogs housegold and Kitchen furniture farming utensils eC.

I further give and bequeath unto the balance of my children to wit Katherine Colyer Samuel B Sherrill Henry Sherrill Monera South, Uriah Sherrill and Adam Sherrill's children that is to say Adam Sherrills children to have their fathers part, four hundred and about twenty six acres being part of two tracts of land, one of two hundred acres entered in the Entry Takers office of Franklin County on the 5th day of Feby 1835 Grant no. 4912 Recorded in the Registers Book of the Mountain District in Book H page 41, the other being part of a tract of land containing two hundred and eighty two ½ acres entered in the Entry Takers office of Franklin County the 1st day of October 1832 Grant No. 4916 Recorded in Registers Office of the Mountain District in Book H, page 45 the other fifty six acres of the tract I propose giving to Mary Louize and Julia South by deed of Gift.

I do appoint Henry Hunt my lawful executor to this my last will and testament hereby revoking all former wills and testaments by me made in testimony whereof I have hereunto set my hand and affixed my seal this 18th day of March 1840
P-143   George D. Sherrill (SEAL)
Signed Sealed and delivered in presence of Danial McClean
Acknowledged to John O Brixey

Be it remembered that I THOMAS H BROWN of the County of Coffee and State of Tennessee being weak in body but perfectly in sences knowing that all men must die do make this my last will and testament that is to say

In the first place I want my body decently buried according to my situation in life.

Second, I want all my Just debts paid as soon as my monies can be collected

3rd. I do give and bequeath unto my beloved wife Mary Brown and my three children namely Elizabeth Brown Hasten Brown

and Ann Brown all of my personal property, my desire is that my
personal property shall be equally devided between the four a-
bove named, Mary my wife and Elizabeth, Haston and Ann, and my
will is that my property shall be kept together and under the
control of my wife Maryk my will is then that my wife Mary
shall give off to my children after having my personal property
valued or when they arrive at the age of twenty one their proportionable part of the personal property bat if my wife should
die or marry I then and in that want her share to her fourth
part of my personal property to be given to her and her dower in
the land at the same time. I then want my executore to sell all
the stock that may be on hand belonging to my three children
above named and take in possession their negroes that fall to
them and hire them out until my above named children mary or become of age of twenty one years.

I want my executors to give them a good english education
out of the proceeds of the hire of the negroes and if it should
not be sufficient any monies on hand in the hands of my executors, and should my wife Mary live single, untill they marry I
want her to give them the same schooling that I have authorized
my executor to give them from the proceeds of my land or the
interest arising from any monies that is in the hands of my executors to sell my two stud horses peacock and Monroe whenever
they think best either privately or publicly and the proceeds
to be loaned out by my executors.

If my wife Mary should die before my children are of age I
want my executors to rent my Land out until they come of age
But should my wife Mary live until they arrive of age they may
sell it or divide it as they see proper but in no wise is my
wife to be intempter or her dower If she is desposed to sell
her dower if the children wishes to sell when they come of age
she is at liberty to sell and go with them if it should be her
choice

If any of my slaves shall so act that they connot be gov-
erned by my wife I want my executors to sell them and buy others or put the money out at interest this I leave with my executors, whichever they think will be the most advantageous to
my children to dispose of them in that way or by hireing them
out if any of my above named children should mary before they
arrive at the age of twenty one I want my wife or executore as
the case may be to give them their part of the perishable property I have in my hands one hundred and eighty four dollars
left by my brother Joseph the school his son Elihue I have
schooled and bought him books and clothes the amount of thirteen dollars leaving the above One hundred and Eighty four dollars in ny hands for my executors to school him or if he will
not go to school I want them to loan out the money so soon as
it comes into their hands, until he arrives to the age of twenty
one,

I do appoint my three friends to execute my last will and
testament, John Brown Sr. Gilbert Brown and Andrew X Brown.

In witness whereof I have set my hand and seal this 12th
day of February 1842   Thomas A. Brown (SEAL)
Signed and sealed in presence of   David Ramsey
                                         Stephen Winton

                   In the name of God Amen
I, WILLIAM BOWDEN of the County of Coffee and State of Tennessee being in sound mind and memory but weak in body do make
this my last will and testament,
      Item lst, My soul I hereby resign to God who gave it and
my body to the dust from whence it came.
      Item 2nd. I do will and bequeath unto my beloved wife Nancy
after my death the plantation Just as it is during my wifes life
for her to do with as she pleases and after her death the plantation where I now live is to belong to my two youngest sons viz.
Frederick McBowden and G. L. Bowden, the names or the negroes
Daniel and Priscella and my son G. L. Bowden I leave two negroes
named Louiza and Ben extra of their share after the death of my
wife, This I do acknowledge to be my last will and testament revoking all former wills by me written or caused to be written,
Given under my hand and seal this 21st day of May 1842
                                         William (X) Bowden (SEAL)
Attest   Daniel Hardaway
                                         Dudley Gunn

P-146   In the name of God Amen
I, MARTHA M. MABRY of the County of Coffee and State of Tennessee do make and publish this my last will and testament hereby
revoking and making void all other wills by me at any time made
      Article lst. I give to my daughter Mary Ann Cunningham the
following property to wit Daniel Critty and Dark, one hundred
and fifty dollars and one half of all my house hold furniture
and effects to his and her heirs forever
      2nd. I give to my daughter Harriot B Mabry the following
property to wit. Jane and Ann, four hundred Dollars and one
half of all my house hold furniture and effects to her and her
heirs forever
      3rd. I give to my brother Wm H. Elliott one thousand dol-
lars in trust for my son Hinehia Mabry hereby vesting my said
Brother Will full power to dispose of said thousand dollars in
any way he may think most advantageous to my said son or pay it
over to him when in the Judgement or my said brother it may be
advisable to do so.
      4th. I give to my son Thomas Elliott Mabry one thousand
dollars to him and his heirs forever
      4th. I give to my son John Mabry one thousand dollars to
him and his heirs forever
      6th. Out of the remainder of my estate if there should be
any my will and desire is that all my Just debts be paid and
if there should be anything still remaining after the payment
of all my Just debts I desire that it be equally devided be-

tween my five children viz. Mary Ann Cunningham Hihehea, John E
Harriott B. and Thomas E. Mabry to them and their heirs forever
P-147 But if there should be no remainder as above out of which
to pay my Just debts or should prove inadequate for that purpose
then my will is that an equal amount be deducted from each lega-
tees share to raise a gund sufficient for that purpose
   7th. I hereby constitute my brother William H. Elliott
Guardian for my sons John E and Thos. E Mabry and my daughter
Harritt B Mabry
   Lastly. I do hereby nominate and appoint my said brother
W. H. Elliott and my son in law John Cunningham Executors to th
this my last will and testament. And my desire is that neither
of them be required to give security upon qualifying as such
   In witness whereof I do to this my last will and testament
set my hand and seal this 2d day of May A. D. One thousand
Eighteen hundred and forty two   Martha M. Mabry (SEAL)
signed sealed and published in our presence and we have subscrib
ed our names hereto in the presence of the testator
                                   L Cunningham
                                   H. B. Davis

               State of Tennessee Coddee County
I, THOMAS BUTLER do make and publish this as my last will and
testament hereby revoking and making void all other wills by me
at any time made
   1st. I direct that my funeral expenses and all my debts
be paid as soon after my death as possible out of any money that
I may die possessed of or that may come into the hands of my executors
   2nd. I give and bequeath to Elizabeth Butler my beloved
wife during her lifetime all of my property that I am in possession of at dating of this my last will and testament
P-148 3rd. I bequeath to Mary Ann Duncan one feather bed, I
will and bequeath to John R Butler my beloved son all of my
goods and chattels, lands and household furniture after the
death of my wife.
   I will and bequeath to Lilburn Butler two doooars also Martha Grant two dollars, also Jane Brown two dollars also George
C Butler two dollars also Jefferson Butler two doooars also
Sarah Turner two Dollars.
   In witness whereof I do to this my will and testament set
my hand and seal this 23d day of September 1839.
                                   Thomas (X) Butler (SEAL)
Signed Sealed and delivered in presence of us
                                   Thomas Parker
                                   Joel O. Thacker
                                   G. Jones

         The last Will and Testament of Jonathan Webster
   I, JONATHAN WEBSTER of Coffee County Tennessee do make or-
ordain and publish this my last will and testament in the man-

ner and form following to wit

1st. I direct that all my Just debts and funeral expenses be paid by my executors as soon after my death as possible out of the proceeds of my landed estate, and the notes I hold on different people, and for the purpose of carrying the clause into effect I fully authorize and empower my executors to sell as much of my lands and such portions thereof as they may think proper, as may be necessary to pay all the demands against my estate which my notes and debts due will not pay

2d. I direct that after the payment of my debts and funeral expenses. My executors shall have power to sell the balance B -149 of my Real Estate that may remain unsold, if in their opinion it shall be neccessary to do so, in order to make a distribution among my heirs

3d. I direct that in the distribution of all the residue of my estate after the payment of all my Just debts as directed in the first clause of this my will, all my children shall share equally but they shall also account for all the advancements either of land money or personal property heretofore made therin, and those who have received most, shall not be entitled to a devision of part of the residue untill all the others are made up equal, And in the distribution to be made the children of my son Joel H Webster deceased, shall stand in the place of and represent their deceased parent and shall account for ad vancements made to them in like manner as my orter legatees

4th. Having already made by a convey in trust to my friend Charles Ready ample provisions for her in this my will

5th. I hereby nominate constitute and appoint my friend Charles Ready of Murgreesbore Executor of this my last will and testament hereby revoking and making void all other wills by me made

In testimony whereof I have hereunto set my hand and seal and published the same this 24th day of October 1842

Jonathon (X) Webster(SEAL)

Signed Sealed and published in presence of us who have witnessed in the presence of the Testator and in presence of each other this 24th day of October 1842

William S. Watteson
James M. Stephens
William S. Norton

P-150 HENRY GORHER WILL
In the name of God Amen

I, HENRY GOHER of the State of Tennessee and Coffee County do make and publish this my last will and Testament hereby revoking and making void all other wills by me at any time made.

1st. I direct that my funeral expenses and all my debts be paid as soon after my death as possible out of any monies I may die possessed of or that may first come into the hands of my executors

2nd. I give and bequeath to my beloved wife Susanna two hundred and twenty five dollars being the amount of money handed

to me by her and by verbal contract entered into by us previous to our intermarrage was to be again given to her my beloved wife Susanna if she should survive me, And also two beds
and furniture and one Stead one good sevisable horse beast of
her own choosing from my stock, one table one book shelf one
clock one chest and one &C. to have and hold during her natural life time and dispose of the same as may seem good to her
provided it be to any one or all of my heirs.

3rd. I give and bequeath to my daughter Nancy Dunaway five
dollars

4th. I give and bequeath to my beloved Grandson Pleasant H.
Halton for and in consideration of the natural love and
affection and for the attention he hath doth and may pay to me
in my old age and afflicted state, the balance of that would be
a lawful distributive share of all my estate to my beloved
Daughter Nancy Dunaway

5th The balance of my heirs I wish to share in my estate
as the laws of my koffy County hath provided
P- 151 Lastly, I make and appoint my beloved son Jesse Gopher
the sole executor of this my last will and Testament

In witness whereof I do to this my will set my hand and
seal this the sixth of January 1843   Henry Gopher (SEAL)
Sighen sealed and delivered in our presence and we have subscribed our names hereto in the presence of the testator this
24 Manuary 1843   George Rpberts
                                       James (X) James

I, HENRY GOPHER having made and published my last will and
testament do make and declare this as a codicle thereto to wit-
First, That my beloved wife Susanna shall have during her
life or widowhood full possession of the house where I now live
with as much land adjoining as will be sufficient for her support and one choice cow and calf one sow and pigs one ewe and
lamb lastly it is my desire that this codicil be attached to
and constitute a part of my will to all interests and purposes
this this 7th day of February A. Dl 1843 Henry Gopher (SEAL)
Signed sealed and published in our presence and we have subscribed our names hereto in the presence of the testator this 7th
day of Feby. 1843   George Roberts
                                       H. R. Gopher

ELIZABETH DOUGLASS WILL
In the name of God Amen

I, ELIZABETH DOUGLASS relict of Will Douglas aged about 56 years
and being in infirm health but sound mind do make this my last
will and testament, that is to say

In the first place I desire all my Just ___ to be paid
P-152 2d. In the consideration of my son Benjamin Douglass having taken care of me since my husbands death I give and bequeath
to him all my personal property now in my possession consisting
of a negro woman Jane and a girl Catherine also all my personal

property on this place and elsewhere

Also I give and bequeath to my son Benjamin all my own divided interest in both the personal and real estate of Bartholome Wood late of Kentucky which property is in the possession of my mother residing near Hopkinsville Kentucky and I do desire my son to see and take possession of my property in Kentucky so soon as my mother may die

I do hereby appoint my son Benjamin my executor to carry into effect this will as to the other children I see proper not to give one cent as they have been fully advanced heretofore

In testimony whereof I do hereunto affix my hand and seal, I am the owner of a childs part of the tract of land on which I now reside that I also give to my son Benjamin but should I only have a right of Dower then I cannot give it after my death

This 9th day of February 1839 Elizabeth (X) Douglass(SEAL)
In presence of us February 9th 1839   J. P. Thompson
Joseph Hamilton

State of Tennessee Coffee County
The last will and testament of JOSEPH WILLIS
I, JOSEPH WILLIS of the State and County aforesaid being In sound and disposing mind and memory and knowing that all men are P-153 bound to die and after death to Judgement and as touching my worldly estate it has pleased God to bless me with I dispose of the same in the following manner that is to say

1st. I will and bequeath to my beloved wife Bitzy Ann Willis all the land belonging to me with all my negroes, horses cattle hogs sheep farming utensils with my wagon also all of my house hold and kitchen furniture all of the above named property is to bring to my beloved wife during her natural life there for my land to be devided equally by her between my three sons the best of the estate to be so divided as to make my daughters equal shares with the sons so that all the children have their proportionable part of my estate

Item 2d. It is my wish and desire that should it be the will of God that my wife should die before the little children are raised and receive their portion of schooling that the children shall choose three disinterested persons whose duty it shall be to see that they have a sufficiency out of the estate for their raising and schooling to make them equal to the other children that when they are all of age all both sons and daughters have their portion of the estate that there be equality

Also it is my will that my executors shall demand and collect all debts and claims Justly due to my estate and that they settle all Just claims against the estate

And lastly I do hereby nominate constitute and appoint my beloved wife and my son John G. Willis Executors to this my last will and testament and it is my wish and desire that any two of the subscribing witnesses making oath in open court shall be sufficient evidence to prove this my last will and testament hereby revoking all other wills by me heretofore made.

signed sealed published and declared by the above named Joseph
p-154 Willis to be his last will and testament in the presence
of us who have hereto subscribed our names as witnesses in the
presence of each other and witnesses in the presence of each
other and the testator on the 1st day of May 1843

Witnesses

Joseph Willis (SEAL)
David Willis
John P. Willis

State of Tennessee Coffee County
The following is the last will and testament of JOHN NELSON
deceased as proven by the oaths of the subscribing witnesses
thereto on the 4th day of September 1843, before the Worshipful
County Court of Coffee County 1843   J. W. Anderson   Clerk
    I, JOHN NELSON of the County of Coffee and State of Tenn-
essee do make and publish this as my last will and testament
hereby revoking and making void all other wills by me at any
other time made
    1st. I direct that my funeral expenses and my debts paid as
soon after my death as possible out of any monies that I may die
possessed of or first coming into the hands of my esecutors
    2d. I give and bequeath unto my wife Lucy, my gray mare,
Margaret one lady saddle and bridle one cow called rose and her
calf with all the household furniture and kitchen furniture and
all my land that lies east of the rever with the meanders of the
river with what little stock of hogs I have, during her natural
life also one axe and two iron wedges, one hoe one grindstone
and one large red heifer one clock and two spinning wheel two
trunks and two boxes one pair of gears and single tree one pair
P-p55 of saddle bags during her natural life
    Lastly I do hereby nominate and appoint James M Vaughan and
Lucy my wife and my daughter Mary Hantcock my executors
    In witness whereof I John Nelson the sd. testator have to
this my will written on one sheet of paper set my hand, and seal
this 13th day of August 1843   John Nelson
signed sealed and published in the presence of the testator and
of each other   Witnesses   William Casey
                                       S. H. D. Duncan
                                       James Winiger
                                       H. L. Duncan

State of Tennessee Coffee County
The following is the last will and testament of John Stiles deceased as proven by the oath of Joseph Fletcher subscribing witness thereto and the handwriting by Jesse P. Nevill the other
subscribing witness before the Worshipful County Court of Coffee
Coffee on the 4th day of March 1844   J. W. Anderson   Clerk
    I, JOHN STILES of the County of Coffee and State of Tennes-
see do make and publish this my last will and testament hereby
revoking and making void all former wills by me at any time here
tofore made

Item 1st. I direct that my body be decently intered at
Mary E Nevills in said county in a manner suitable to my condition in life and as to such worldly estate as it has pleased
the Lord to trust me with I despose of the same as follows
    1st. I direct that all my debts and funeral expenses be
paid as soon after my decease as possible out of any money
that I may die possessed of or may first come into the hands of
my executors from any portion of my estate Real or personal
P-156 2nd. I give and bequeath to my daughter Mary E. Nevill
two beds and furniture one bay mare 6 head of cattle and one
still
    3rd. I give and bequeath to my son John Stiles the sum of
five dollars in money
    4th. I give and bequeath to my son Leroy Stiles five dol-
lars in money
    And I do hereby make ordain and appoint my daughter Mary
E Nevill executrix of this my last will and testament
    In witness whereof I John Stiles the said testator have
to this my will set my hand and seal this 6th day of November
one thousand eight hundred and forty one   John Stiles (SEAL)
signed sealed and published in the presence of us who have
subscribed in the presence of the testator and each other
Witnesses   John Fletcher
                                        Jesse P. Nevill

The following is the last will and testament of James Sutton
deceased as proven by the oaths of Eli Petty and Robt. M Petty
subscribing withesses thereto before the worshipful County
Court of Coffee County on the 6th day of May 1844
                            J. W. Anderson   Clerk
I, JAMES SUTTON do make and publish this my last will and testament hereby revoking and making void all other wills by me at
any time made
    1st. I direct that my funeral expenses and all my debts be
paid as soon after my death as possible out of any money that
I may die possessed of or may first come into the hands of my
executors
P-157 2nd. I give unto my beloved wife Polly Sutton the farm
whereon I now live with all the household and kitchen furniture
and farming tools and all of my stock of all kinds during her
life or widowhood and at her death the said farm where I now
live on my will is that my son Hugh Sutton shall have it as to
the amount of two hundred and fifty acres including the improve
ments at the age of twenty one that is if my wife is dead or
single, she is not to be dispossessed of the dwelling house and
so much of the land as will be sufficient for her support
    3rd. My will is that all my heirs shall be made equal as
near as possible and in order to show my intentions I will my
daughter Elizebeth Jones one horse saddle and bridle one cow
and calf one sow and pigs one ewe and lambs one bed and furniture one tract of land worth three hundred dollars which she

has received

I will to my son John Sutton one horse saddle and bridle one cow and calf one sow and pig one ewe and lambs one bed and furniture one tract of land worth three hundred dollars which he has received

I will to my son William Sutton one horse saddle and bridle one cow and calf one sow and pig one ewe and lambs one bed and furniture one tract of land worth three hundred dollars which he has received

I will to my son Jacob Sutton one horse saddle and bridle one tract of land worth three hundred dollars which he had received

I will to my daughter Catherine Morrow one horse saddle and bridle one cow and calf one sow and pigs one bed and furniture all of which she has received

I will to my son Saml K Sutton one saddle and bridle, all he has received
P-158 I will to my daughter Nancy Jane Sutton one saddle and bridle which is all she has received.

My son Hugh James has not received any thing my will is that the balance of my heirs to wit-- Jacob Sutton Catherine Morrow and Saml K Sutton and Nancy Jane Sutton Hugh James Sutton be made equal in land and in every respect with John Sutton Elizabeth Jones and William Sutton and at the death of my wife if there should be any remainder after all are made equal the balance to be equally devided among all the heirs

Lastly I do hereby nominate and appoint my son Jacob Sutton my executor

In witness whereof I do to this my last will set my hand and seal this 18th day of April 1844   James Sutton (SEAL)
Signed sealed and published in our presence and we do subscribe our names hereto in the presence of the testator this 18th day of April 1844 Witnesses   Eli Petty
                                                 R M Petty

A Copy of the Noncupative will of ROBT PETTERSON Deceased was proven by the oath of Elias Teal and David D. Smith subscribing witnesses thereto in open Court on the 4th day of June 1844
                                    J. W. Anderson Clerk
This last will and testament of Robt. Patterson deceased
P-159   My will is as follows namely

1st. that my debts all be paid and relation to the Contract that myself and David Smith have made in relation to tending my farm and raising to be continued until the time expires or until Mr Smith wishes to give it up and that my son John Patterson stand in my place to said contract and at the expiration of said contract with Mr. Smith I wish my son John to proceed to sell all my property with my land and divide the proceeds equal ly between all six of my children namely John, Susanna, Mary, Thomas, Elizabeth and Abraham after retaining to himself the necessary expenses of having this business all attended to

Done on the 25th day of April 1844
Signed in presence of Elias Teal and David D Smith Witnesses

The last will and testament of Louis Taylor as proven by the
oaths of Michael Stephens and Branson James in the County Court
of Coffee County on Monday the first day of July 1844,

J. W. Anderson Clerk

I, LOUIS TAYLOR of Coffee County and State of Tennessee
being weak of body but of sound mind and desposing memory thank
to God for his mercies knowing the mortality of my body all
that it is appointed unto all men once to die, do make and ordain this my last will and testament hereby revoking and making
void all other wills by me made

1st. And princably of all I bequeath my soul to God who
gave it and my body to the dust, to be buried in a christian
burial at the descretion of my executors and as to such worldly
goods as it has pleased God to give me I give devise and dispose of in the following manner and form viz:

1st. I request and desire that all my debts as soon after
P-160 my death as monies come into the hands of my executor
shall be paid

2nd. I give and bequeath my gray horse to my dearly beloved daughter Evy Collins wife of Mr. William Collins

3rd. I give and bequeath to my dearly beloved daughter Nancy King wife of Jorden King one bay horse.

4th. I give and bequeath unto my grand children Louis Taylor and Rhoda Taylor the son and daughter of my dearly beloved
son James Taylor my bay mare and colt which I desire after my
death my Said son James take possession of and use

5th. I give and bequeath to my dearly beloved daughter
Ferigy Taylor my walnut chest

6th. I give and bequeath my beloved son in law William
Collins my interest in a two horse wagon and breaching that we
are gointly concerned in

7th. I give and bequeath to my beloved daughter E Leuiza
Burton wife of James Burton my patent clock

8th. I give to my dearly beloved son George Taylor my bed
and furniture which I desire to remain at William Collins after my death until it is applied for by said George Taylor or
his authorized attorney

9th. I give and bequeath to my beloved son John L Taylor
one wagon worth one hundred dollars and one note on W. A. and W
Hickerson for one hundred and thirty dollars which has already
had, as to my other goods that I may die sired or possessed of
I give to my executor for the trouble he will necessary incur
in carrying into affect this my last will and testament
P-161 10th. And lastly I do hereby constitute and appoint William Collins Sr. executor of this my last will and testament,
made and published by me this 18th day of May in the year of
our Lord Eighteen hundred and forty four Louis Taylor (SEAL)
Signed in presence of us Michael Stephens Branson James

Copy of the last will and testament of Jacob Hoover as
proven by the oath of Matthew Hoover and Martin Hoover subsrib-
ing witnesses thereto in County Court of Coffee County 7th October 1844

I Jacob Hoover do make and publish this as my last will
and testament hereby revoking and making void all other wills
by me at any time made

1st. I direct that my funeral expenses and all my Just
debts be paid as soon after my death as possible out of any
money that I may die possessed of or that may first come into
the hands of my executors

2nd. I give aand bequeath unto my son Mathias Hoover one
negro boy about five years old named Caleb

3rd. I give and bequeath to my son Simeon Hoover one negro man named Jacob about 22 years old

4th. I give and bequeath to my son Eulias Hoover one negro firl about eighteen years old named Dinah and her increase

5th. I give and bequeath to my son Martin Hoover one negro man about twenty five years old named Frank

6th. I give and bequeath to my daughter Elizabeth Rowlings
and her jusband Louis J. Rowlings one negro man named Joe about
forty years old.

7th. I give and bequeath to my wife Polly Hoover one negro boy about to years old named John.
P162-8th. I give and bequeath to my son Henry Hoover one negro
woman named Clary about fifty years old.

9th. I give and bequeath to my wife Polly Hoover my part
of a tract of land myself and Mathias Hoover bought of the
heirs of William Rowlings

10th. All my household and kitchen furniture stock and
farming tools I wish to be equally devided between my wife Polly Hoover and my son Julius Hoover

11th. I give and bequeath all the land I am now possessed
of or may be possessed of at my death after paying my Just
debts, to Julius Hoover and

Lastly I do nominate and appoint John B McGuire and Lewis
Horde executors

In witness whereof I do this day set my hand and eeal this
24th May 1843   Jacob Hoover (SEAL)
                                  Mathius Hoover
                                  Martin Hoover

The following is the last will and testament of C. S.
ROACH Deceased as proven in open Court 2 Decr. 1844

I, CHARLES ROACH do make and publish this my last will and
testament hereby revoking and making void all other wills by me
at any time made

1st. I direct that my funeral expenses and all my debts be
paid as soon after my death as possible out of any money I may
die possessed of or that may first come into the hands of my
executors

2d. I give and bequeath to him his mother Elizabeth
Roach a Phebe Brown his sister her lifetime and at his mothers
death a certain negro slave girl by the name of Martha
P-163 I give the said girl to my sister Phebe Brown and to her
bodily heirs forever the said girl to wait as much on one of
them as the other until my mothers death also after all my Just
debts are paid I want my land sold and equally devided between
Phebe Brown Georger her brother William her brother also

In witness whereof I do to this my last will and testament
set my hand and seal this 2d. day of October 1844

                        Charles L (X) Roach(SEAL)
Signed sealed and published and we have subscribed our names
hereto in the presence of this testator this 2nd day of October
Witnesses   Henry Brewer
                                 John Brewer

I, ROBERT S. RAYBURN do make and publish this as my last
will and testament hereby revoking and making void all other
wills by me at any time made

1st. I direct that my guneral expenses and all my debts be
paid as soon after my death as possible out of any money that I
may die possessed of or may first come into the hands of my executors

2nd. It is my desire that my property of whatever kind remain in the hands of my beloved wife during her widowhood or
natural life for the purpose of raising and educating my children

3rd. It is my desire that whenever any of my children marry or become of age that my executors distribute to them such
portion of property or money as to them may seem proper keeping
a correct account so that finally each child may receive an e-
quitable share

4th.It is my desire that should my beloved wife ever inter
marry whe shall receive a childs part of all my property both
P-164 real and personal and at her death to return to my heirs

5th. It is my desire that sholuld my beloved wife die during her widowhood that my personal property be sold and equally
distributed among my heirs and that my land and slaves be either devided or sold as my executors may think best for the interest of the heirs and the proceeds equally devided among them

6th. It is my desire that my desire that my slaves Cleo
remain in the family and should she at any time become a charge
I want her maintained of of the estate

7th. And lastly I nominate and appoint my beloved wife Mary
with Adam Rayburn and Andrew Maxwell my executrix and executors
none of whom are required to enter into bond and security until
the intermatriage or death of my wife

In witness whereof I do to this my last will and testament
set my hand and esal this the 31th day of December 1844

                        Robt S Rayburn (SEAL)
signed sealed and published in our presence and we have subscribed our names hereto in the presence of the testator the date

above written Witnesses, W. A. Waterson J. A. Brantley
     The above is a true Copy of the last will and testament
of R. S. Rayburn decd. as proven 7th day of April 1845
                              J. W. Anderson Clerk
                                of Coffee County

p-165 Copy of the last will and testament of Elizabeth Wallace
as proven May 6 1845
     I, ELIZABETH WALLACE do make and publish this as my last
will and testament hereby revoking and making void all other
wills by me at any time made
     1st. I direct that my funeral expenses and all my debts
be paid as soon after my death as possible out of any money
that I may die possessed of or may first come into the hands of
my executors
     2nd. I give and bequeath to my daughter Nancy three negroes
Lucy Alexander and Mary
     3rd. I give and bequeath to my daughter Elizabeth Lambert
and her heirs three negroes Jacob Marthae and Jim
     4th. I desire that the remainder of my perishable property
be sold the executor and the proceeds to be equally devided as
above
     5th. I further desire my land to be equally devided be-
tween my two daughters or sold by the executor and the proceeds
to be equally devided as above
     Lastly I do hereby nominate and appoint Thomas W. Mason my
executor this 9th day of April 1845   Elizabeth (X) Wallace
                                                      (SEAL)
Signed sealed and published in our presence and we have subscri
bed our names hereto in presence of the testator this 9th day
of April 1845 Witnesses, James McMichael,William McMichael

State of Tennessee
     Pleas: At a Circuit Court began and held for the County of
Coffee at the Court house in the town of Manchester on the 4th
Monday the same being the 27th day of June 1842

P-166   In the name of God Amen
     I, DUNCAN NEIL of the County of Coffee and State of Tenne-
ssee being weak in body but of sound and perfect mind and memory, considering the uncertainty of this mortal and being of
sound &C. Blessed be almighty God for the same do make and publish this my last will and testament in manner and form following that is to say
     Item 1st, I give and bequeath my soul unto God who gave it
     Item 2d. I give and bequeath unto my beloved wife Betty
the sum of one hundred and fifty dollars with her bed and bedding
     Item 3rd. I do also give and bequeath unto my son James
Neil the plantation where I now live on with all my lands on
the south side of Duck River running to John Carrolls Spring
Branch

I also will and bequeath to my beloved wife Betsey her life estate on the land while she remains a widow or see cause to stay on the land then and in that case the profits arising from the land ceases to be hers and the profits arising from the land to go to my two youngest James Neil and Angeline Neil and they are to be educated on the profits arising therefrom P-167 I also will and bequeath unto Elizabeth Neil her life estate on the land where I now live with wood and water and land for any cultivation she sees proper to live on the land then and in that case her claim or claimes to cease on said land,

And all my moveable property to be sold and the proceeds devided among the following heirs excepting my servant John who shall not be sold under six years after my decease but shall remain as a slave on the plantation for the benefit of the family who resides there and then to be sold and to be desposed of as the balance of the property

I do also make Elizabeth Neil my lawful heir to her part of the property that is to be sold. Livewise Thomas Neil Ellen Campbell Alexander Neil Oldfield Nancy Oldfield Susan Hardaway Rachael Yell Angeline Neil all my lawful heirs as for William Neil and James Neil they have received their part excepting five dollars each

I appoint my son Alexander Neil Administrator of this my last will and testament hereby revoking all former wills by me made

In witness whereof I have hereunto set my hand and seal the 28th day of November 1840   Duncan Neil (SEAL) Signed sealed and published by the above named Duncan Neil to be his last will and testament in the presence of us who have hereunto subscribed our names as witnesses in the prexence of the testator   Attests--Daniel Hardaway, John Penn

P-168 State of Tennessee
Coffee County
Pleas: At a County Court began and held for the County of Coffee at the Court house in the town of Manchester on the 27th day of June A. D. 1842 Present the Hon. Andrew J Marchbanks Judge of the 13th Judicial Circuit of said State,

And afterwards to wit on Friday the 5 day of said term the same being the 1st day of July 1842 The Hon Andrew J. Marchbanks present when the following proceedings were held to wit: Alex. Neil Exr of Duncan Neil Dd.
vs
Bary
Hardaway and Susan his wife Moses Yell and Rachael his wife David Oldfield and Mary his wife and John Campbell and Ellen his wife Charles Oldfield and Nancy his wife and Wm Neil heirs at law of Duncan Neil Deceased this day came the parties by their attorneys and thereupon came a Jury of good and lawful men to wit Asa M Elkner John Kennedy Thomas Cavert NC Phillips Crisley Messick Eli Emmick David Wiser Joseph J Patton Isaac A

Gillis William Hodge Robt Carlisle and Geo. W. Chapman who being duly tried and sworn well and truly to try the issue join-
ed between the parties and to render a true verdict according
to the evidence upon their oath do say that they find so much
of the paper-writing purposing to be the last will and testament of Duncan Neil deceased in the pleadings in this case mentioned as assmues to devise the lands therein mentioned not to
P-169 be the last will and testament of Duncan Neil Deceased
but the Jury further says that they find so much of said paper
writing as assumes to despose of the personal property therein
mentioned to be the last will and testament of said Duncan Neil
Deceased

Whereupon it is considered by the Court that the same be
certified upon said will to the end that it may be recorded in
the proper office that it may be recorded in the proper office
and that the defendants recover against the plaintiff their
costs about their suit in this behalf expended, for which let
execution issue

State of Tennessee
Coffee County

I, WILLIS BLANTON Clerk of the Circuit Court for said
County do certify that the foregoing is a true and perfect
transcript of the record od said Court in said cause all of
which remain of second in my office

Given under my hand and private seal (there being no seal
of said court) at office this 17th day of September A D 1845
and the 70 year of American Independence Willis Blanton Clerk
Recorded 19th September 1845 J. W. Anderson, Clerk of the
County Court of C County

State of Tennessee
Coffee County

The following is the last will and testament of John Hickerson Decd. in Open Court A. M. Holt and D. V. Davidson subscribing witnesses thereto and ordered to be recorded
J. W. Anderson Clerk

I, JOHN HICKERSON do make and publish this as my last will
and testament hereby revoking all former wills by me at any time
made
P-170 Item 1st. I wish my executors hereinafter named to pay al
all my Just debts so soon after my death as possible

Item 2nd. I wish my wife to have my Hazel Patch lands
which includes all the lands that adjoins the old Hazel Patch
place during her life and at her death my will is that they be
equally devided between my two youngest sons John W and Litle
Hickerson which I value to them at four thousand dollars in the
distribution of my estate

Item 3rd. My further will and wish is that all my negroes
and other property with my wife during her lifetime subject to

her control and that the labor of my negroes over and above
that may be necessary to the support of my wife go to the payment of what debts I may owe at my death if however what debts
are coming to me and the proceeds of the labor of my negroes
are not sufficient to pay my debts by the time my executors are
compelled to meet them then they are directed to sell such of t
the negroes or other property as may be necessary for such purpose and my executors are directed to take all such steps and
do all such things as may be necessary to promote the comfort o
of my said wife and enhance the interest of the estate

Item 4th. My will is that after the death of my wife (or
during her life she and my executors consenting thereto) the
balance of whatever property real or personal that I may die
seized and possessed of be equally between the following persons (each and first accounting for whatever advancements they
P-171 may have received heretofore, and my two youngest sons
first accounting for the sum of two thousand dollars each the
value of the land devided to them in this will) to wit, Effiee
Powers Delphis Powers Cynthea Bowden William P. Hickerson
Charles Hickerson John W. Hickerson Lille Hickerson Lucy Timmons wife of Ambrose Timmons her portion I give to her for her
own seperate use free from the contracts of her said husband
and for the support of herself and children also the portion
or Eliza Aldridge to be for her support and for her own seperate use free from the influence and control of her uusband
John Aldrige the two last named devises are also first to account for any advancements heretofore made to them or their
husbands

Item 5th. I do hereby nominate and appoint Thomas Powers
and W. P. Hickerson executors of this my last will and testament. Signed and dated this 16th day of July 1845
                                        John Hickerson (SEAL)
Signed and sealed by the testator in the presence of us and
subscribed by us in the presence of the testator and in presence of the testator and in presence of each other this 17th
day of July 1845   Witnesses   A. M. Holt
                                     D. V. Davidson

The following is the last will and testament of JAMES
CUNNINGHAM deceased as proven in the County Court of Coffee
County of the 1st Monday in December 1845 and ordered by said
Court to be recorded   J. W. Anderson Clerk

In the name of God Amen, I, JAMES CUNNINGHAM a citizen of
Coffee County and State of Tennessee do hereby make and publish
P-172 this my last will and testament that is to say

1st. Whereas previous to the intermarriage of myself and
wife then Polly or Mary Hollinsworth widow of James Hollinsworth deceased, we entered into a marriage contract in and by
which among other things It was stipulated that my said wife
at and after my death should have the power to dispose of her

land and the following negroes by will to wit: Alfred Anthony
Matilda and Micy and their increase being at present three in
number to wit Sam and Preston sons of Matilda and George son of
Micy

The true interest and meaning of which contract signed and
sealed by the parties but not registered was that I was only
the have a life estate in the lands and negroes and that upon
my decease all the right and title to said land and negroes was
to revert to my said wife or her lawful heirs

Now I do hereby satify and confirm said contract to all in
tent and purposes and I do hereby relinquish to my said wife
and her heirs all title and claims which I may have to said
lands and the negroes aforesaid with full power to my said wife
to dispose of the same by will or otherwise in such a manner as
she may think proper, and being desirous to make other provisions for the comfort and independent support of my said wife
during her life or widowhood which she so wells deserves at my
hands for the very faithful and tender discharge of her conjugal
duties as well as those of the adopted mother of my children I
P-173 do hereby give and bequeath to her during her life or
widowhood all the arable or inclosed lands on my two hundred
acre occupant claim on the south side of the creek with the exception of the corner field which contains about fifteen acres
together with all the building thereon

Also my threshing machine and cotton gin on the north side
of the creek with a sufficientcy of timber for all useful purposes

I also give and bequeath to my said wife the use of the fo
following property during the term aforesaid to wit: one choice
wagon and gearing, four horses to be selected by her out of my
stock one half of my stock of cattle and hogs the whole of my
stock of cattle and hogs the whole of my stock of sheep, she
giving to my daughter Sinai Harris one third of the wool of
said sheep after the same should be sheared to the sole and seperate use of my said daughter and her children, three choice be
beds bedsteads and furniture, as much of the household and kitchen furniture as she may need, one choice bureau my loom and
family spinner with all the articles belonging to the same my
family bible and testament a sufficiency of the farming tools
to carry on the farm together with such part of the shop tools
as may be necessary provided bowever that it is the true intent
and meaning of the devise in cause in relation to the use of th
the land that her right thereto is to continue so long only as
it may be the pleasure to remain thereon, should she remove
therefrom then the same is to vest in those in remainder as
hereafter provided

I also give and bequeath to my said wife apart by my executor a sufficiency of corn wheat oats or other grain hay or
P-174 fodder for the support of her family and stock one year

Item 2d. The several tracts of land on which I now reside
containing near six hundred acres I devise to my son Rowley

Cunningham and my daughter Sinai Harris and her children to be
devided between them as follows to wit beginning at the south
East corner of my two hundred acre occupant claim or tract
running with the south boundary line of the same forty poles
thence north paralel with the eastern boundary line of the
same to the south eastern boundary line of the same to the
south boundary line of said tract thence with said line thirty
poles thence northwardly parallel with Henry Golchers west
boundary line through a tract of land I purchased of Anderson
& Strother to the north boundary line of the same thence last
with said to Henry Gotchers north west corner thence south
with said Gotchers west boundary line to the north boundary
line of my two hindred acre occupant tract thence east with
said line to the north east corner of said occupant tract
thence round with Gotcher and other lines to the beginning, including the Thompson tract, all the land included in said lines
I give and bequeath to my said son Rowley Cunningham

I estimate the value of said land at thirteen hundred dollars together with four hundred and sixty one dollars already
advanced makes the sum of seventeen hundred and sixty one dollars

I also give and bequeath to my said son Rowley Cunningham
one negroe man now in his possession named Samsone which said
negroe I give him over and above an equal share on account of
his being deaf and dumb from his birth

I also give and bequeath to my said son Rowley Cunningham
my secratary and book case of which no account is to be taken
and if one share should amount to more than seventeen hundred
and sixty one dollars then and in that case he is to be made
equal with the rest of my legatees

Item 3rd. I give and bequeath to my daughter Sinai Harris
all the lands west of the west boundary line of the lands devised to my son Rowley to the sole and seperate use and for
the support of herself and family during her life and at her
death I give and bequeath the remainder in fee simple to the
children of my said daughter and their heirs forever I estimate the value of said lands to my daughter and her children
at two thousand dollars if the value of said land should not
be equal but if it or the property advanced to Rowley should
amount to more than one share, they are not to pay any thing
back to the rest of the legatees

And whereas upon the marrige of my said daughter I gave
her a negro girl named Emily who has been lately sold under execution to satisfy the debts of her husband at which sale I be-
came the purchaser and have again given her to my said daughter
over and above the rest of the legatees on account of her being
deaf and dumb and in any devision of my estate neither her nor
her heirs are to be charged with said girl (now a woman) upon
the first or second gift.

Item 4th. The balance of my estate both real and personal
I give and bequeath to my children and grandchildren hereinafter

P-176 named to be equally devided among them that is to say to
the widow and children of my deceased son Wiley Cunningham, I
give one share, Mark Cunningham one share, my son John Cunningham one share, My son William Cunningham one share my daughter
Elizabeth Crocker one share my son Henry Cunningham one share
provided that in the devision of the slaves I expressly enjoin
it upon my executor as well as my children not to seperate the
men and their wives without their consent but if necessary in
the alottment and Devision to require a legatee or legatees
getting a man and wife if more than their share to pay the
oveplus to the others and provided further that in making the
devision of the property each legatee is to bring unto hotch
potch the amount of money and property heretofore advanced to
them of which I have indeavered with a view to do equal and im-
partial Justice among my children to keep an account up to this
date they have received as follows and are to be charged accordingly to wit.
     My son Wiley Cunningham one hundred and seventy five dol-
lars including a note I hold on him for one hundred and ninety
four dollars for which no interest is to be charged and also including one hundred dollars sent his wife since his death by her
son James. My son Mark Cunningham five hundred and eighty
eight dollars. My son John Cunningham nine hundred and twenty
two dollars. My son William nine hundred and eight dollars my
P-177 son Henry Cunningham seven jundred and seventy nine dollars. To my daughter Elizabeth Crocker I have advanced a negro
girl Arminda at the price of one hundred and seventy five dollars also six hundred dollars in other advancements since
     Item 5th. To enable my executor to make a devision of my
estate as herein divected he is hereby fully authorized and em-
powered to make sale of such of my real estate as may not be
especially devised which as well as now recollected consist only of a tract of land of fifty acres on or near the head of Elk
river one other tract of sixty four acres in civil destrict no.
8 also one other tract of Eighty acres in District no. 8
     Lastly I appoint my son William Cunningham executor of
this my last will and testament hereby revoking all former wills
     Witness my hand and seal this 27th day of August 1845
                         James Cunningham (SEAL)
Signed sealed published and delivered by the testator as and
for his last will and testament in our presence who subscribed
as witnesses in his presence Witnesses, Daniel McClean
                              Benj. F. Holleims
                              William B Williams

State of Tennessee
Coffee County
     At a County Court began and held for Coffee County on the
1st Monday of December 1845 this last will and testament of
James Cunningham deceased was produced in open Court by the

executor therein named and proven by the oaths of Dan'l Mc-
Clean and Benj. F. Hollins subscribing witnesses thereto and
ordered to be recorded   J. W. Anderson Clerk

P-178 I, JACOB HOOVER do make and publish this my last will and
testament hereby revoking and making void all other wills by me
at any time made

1st. I direct that my funeral expenses and all my debts be
paid as soon after my death as possible out of any money that I
may die possessed of or that may first come into the hands of m
my executors

2nd. I give and bequeath to my son Mathias Hoover one negro boy about five years old named Caleb.

3rd. I give and bequeath to my son Julius Hoover one negro
girl about Eighteen years old named Dinah and her increase

4th. I geve and bequeath to my son Simeon Hoover one negro
man named Jacob about twenty two years old

5th. I give and bequeath to my son Martin Hoover one negro
man about twenty five years old named Frank Frank

6th. I give and bequeath to my daughter Elizabeth Rowling
one negro man named Joe about forty years old

7th. I give and bequeath to my wife Polly Hoover one negro
boy about two years old named John

8th. I give and bequeath to my son Henry Hoover one negro
woman named Clary about fifty years old

9th. I give and bequeath to my wife Polly Hoover my part o
of a tract of land my self and Mathias Hoover bought of the
heirs of William Rowling

10th. All my household and kitchen furniture stock and
farming tools I wish to be equally devided between my wife Polly
Hoover and my son Julius Hoover

11th. I give and bequeath all the land I am now possessed
of or may be possessed of at my death after paying my Just debts
to Julius Hoover

And lastly I do nominate and appoint John B. McGuire and
Lewis Harrell executors

In witness whereof I do this day set my hand and seal this
24th day of May 1843   Jacob Hoover (SEAL)
                                        Mathias Hoover
                                        Martin (X) Hoover

State of Tennessee
    Pleas: At a Circuit Court began and held for Coffee Co
County at the Court house in the town of Manchester on the
fourth Monday the same being the 27th day of October A D 1845
and the 70teith year of American Independence

    Rresent the Hon. Saml Anderson Judge &C. hereby inter-
change of siding with Hon Andrew J. Marchbanks Judge of the 13th
Judicial Circuit of said State

    And afterwards to wit at the same term the same being on
the 3rd day of November 1845 the Hon. Saml Anderson Judge &C.

Present
        The following proceedings were had to wit:
Julius Hoover
VS   Issue Devi Sen it vel non
Henry Hoover
        Ephriam Hoover Samuel Bingham and wife Ann, William G.
Bingham and wife Mary Christopher Hoover and Simeon Hoover
        This day came the parties by their attorneys and thereup-
on came a Jury of Good and Lawful men to wit:
        Robt. M Haggard Henry Powers S Banks Thomas Allison Thomas
Anderson Henry Brown William Towry David Ralph David Simpson
P-180 James P. Daniel John Bryant and John Thompson who being
elected tried and sworn the truth to speak upon this issue Join-
ed upon their oath do say that the paper writing in the pleadings mentioned purporting to be the last will and testament of
Jacob Hoover deceased is his last will and testament so far as
it relates to the personally which were of the said Jacob Hoover
deceased, but it is not the last will and testament of said Jacob Hoover deceased so far as it relates to the real estate
        It is therefore considered by the Court that it be certifi-
ed to the County Court for probate so far as it relates to the
personality and no further and that the plaintiff recover
against the defendants his costs by him his suit in this behalf
expended and that execution issue

State of Tennessee
Coffee County
        I, WILLIS BLANTON Clerk of the Circuit Court of Coffee
County do certify that the foregoing is a true and perfect transcript of the record and Judgement in the case of Julius C Hoover
against Henry Hoover and others determined in said Court all of
which remain of record in my office
        Given under my hand and private seal (their being no seal
of said Court)
        Done at office this 8th day of Decr. in the year of our
Lord one thousand eight hundred and forty five and the 70 year
of American Independence   Willis Blanton Clerk
                                              (SEAL)

P-181   In the name of God Amen
I, CLAYBURN HART of the County of Coffee and State of Tennessee
being weak in body but of sound mind and disposing memory knowing the mortality of my body and that it is appointed unto all
men once to die do make and ordain this my last will and testament hereby revoking and making void all other wills by me at
any time made
        1st. And principally of all I recommend my soul to God who
gave it and my body to the dust to be buried in a decent and
Christian like manner at the discretion of my executrix, and as
to such worldly goods with which it has pleased God to bless me
I give and bequeath in the following manner and form,

Item 1st. It is my will and desire that all my just debts shall be paid after my death out of any money that may come to the hands of my executrix.

Item 2nd. I give and bequeath unto my dearly beloved wife Celia Harp all the estate I may die sized and possessed of both real and personal (after paying my debts as aforesaid) during her material life or widowhood

Item 3rd. It is my desire and will after the marriage or death of my said wife as the case may be that my estate if any there be, be equally devided between my grand children legitimate children of Alex Harp and Nancy Howard except Celia Ann Elizabeth daughter of Alezander Harp who I desire to have over and above the equal share, one feather bed and furniture one cow and calf

Item 4th. I do hereby constitute and appoint my wife Celia Harp executrix of this my last will and testament

In witness whereof I have hereunto set my hand and seal this 22nd day of January a. D. 1846   Clayburn (X) Harp (SEAL)
P-182 Witnessed by us in the presence of the testator
Michael Stephens
Moses M. Cass

State of Tennessee
Coffee County

At a County Court began and deld for the County of Coffee on the 1st Monday the 2nd day of February 1846 this last will and testament of Clayburn Harp was produced in open Court by the executrix therein named and proven by the oaths of Michael Stephens and Moses M. Cass subscribing witnesses thereto and ordered to be recorded   J. W. Anderson Clerk

I, JOHN HARRIS GARRITT do make and publish this my last will and testament

1st. I direct that my funeral expenses and all my debts be paid as soon after my death as possible out of any money that I may die possessed of or may first come into the hands of my executors

2d. I give and bequeath to my dear wife Belinda the land with its appertenances that I am possessed of that is the Martin seat with one other tract Known by the Brown place, the deed for the tract is not registered, for a further discription of the home tract refer to the Registers office of Bedford County, with all the books and stationary including clothes as well as my stock of horses cattle hogs and sheep with all outstanding debts and with all the stock of grain and forage now on hand with the P-183 whole crop of Bacon that I am now or at my death possessed of with all my farming utensils, and my blacksmith tools that it will be prudent shortly after my death to sell off, so much of my sotck with the blacksmith tools as will be sufficient to pay all my liabilities the residue of my property I will to remain as fund to rear cloth_ and educate my children and recom-

mend my wife under all changing scenes that may be her lot to wi
witness to reserve in her own possession a sufficiency for the
above purpose until they are raised and educated, after that
she is or after her death to make an equal devision of what my
estate may remain among our children, in the event of her death
before the children are raised I wll that the property be sold
and the proceeds be placed in the hands of a guardian to be
appointed for the purpose, In the event of her marriage it is
my wish for her still retain the care of the property and the
children.

But I will that she secure the little estate for the above
purposes by bond and sufficient security before said intended
marriage. I also direct that my wife may sell the Brown place
and the proceeds be reserved in her hands for the general _____
of the family

And Lastly I do hereby nominate and appoint my wife Belinda
my executrix to this my last will and testament with her brother Robt. Wilson as executor   Johnson Harris Garritt(SEAL)
Signed sealed and published in our presence and we have subscribed our names hereto in the presence of the testator this
8th day of Apl 1846
Attests   J. Walker
                                 Thomas Powers

P-184State of Tennessee
Coffee County

At a County Court began and held for the County of Coffee
on the first Monday the ___ day of ___ 1846, thsi last will and
testament of Johnson H Garrett was produced in open Court by
the oaths of James Walker and Thomas Powers subscribing witnesses thereto and ordered to be recorded
                                 J. W. Anderson Clerk

                    In the Name of God Amen
I, EDMOND KEELING being feeble in body but of disposing memory
do make and constitute this to be my last will and testament
revoking all others

1st. I will and bequeath that out of the effects of my estate all my Just debts and my funeral expenses included shall
be paid

2nd. I will and bequeath my negro by John to my two sons
John and Elsy but that he shall remain with the family for their
support until the youngest child becomes of age or until my
wife should marry It is then my wish that my two sons shall despose of him as they think proper

3rd. I will and bequeath all the rest of my effect of what
ever kind to my wife to dispose of as she may think best

Lastly I nominate and appoint James M Avant as the executor
of this my last will and testament

Given under my hand and seal this 8th day of January 1846
                                 Edmond (X) Keeling

p-185 In presence of J.C. Gooch, Joseph Mason, Jno. C. Kirkpatrick

State of Tennessee
Coffee County
    At the County Court began and held for the County of Cof-
fee at the Court house in the town of Manchester the foregoing
last will and testament of E. B. Kelling was produced in open
Court and proven by the oaths of Joseph Mason and Jno. C. Kirkpatrick subscribing witnesses thereto and ordered to be recorded Witness my hand at Office this 6th day of July 1846
                         J. W. Anderson Clerk
                         By Jas Darnell D. C.

State of Tennessee
Coffee County November 6th 1846
    Be it known and remembered that DAVID MONTGOMERY a citi-
zen of the above state and County departed this life on the 5th
day of the above month without having embodied his will and
given it form according to the ordinary rule by the cause of
his sudden attack and pain of his desease but having expressed
his will verbally during his late attack of sickness to his
children and to some of his neighbors and when that expression
is compared with his former expression on the same subject to
S. P. Montgomery his adopted son they are the same in relation
to the distributions of his property and the payment of his out
standing debts and whatever he is bound for which is in substance as follows:
    1st. At sundry times to sundry times to Sandyville, he
wished his three daughters at home that lived with him to enjoy an equal share of his worldly effects or an equal distrubi-
tion of his property after after his debts were paid and whatsoever he was bound for, that he had given his other children
P-186 some help and now wished his home daughters that were un-
married to have the balance in his possession after the debts
shall have been paid as above stated and on his late illness
of which he died stated in presence and stated in the hearing o
of Margaret Broomfield and Caroline Short that he would have
been glad to have lived and settled his affairs more satisfac-
tory but that now he beleived his days were numbered and must
leave the world, but is was his wish first to have all his
debts paid and whatsoever there should be left of his substance
that it be equally devided between my three female children
living with me at home which I understood to be Cynthia and
Easter and Susan Montgomery and it being requested and deemed
most fit, first that William Montgomery be appointed administrator and Susan Montgomery administratrix to the foregoing
    In testimony whereof we have hereunto set our hands this
day and year above written Attest   Sandyville P Montgomery
                              Margaret Broomfield
                              Caroline (X) Short

State of Tennessee
Coffee County
    At a County Court began and held for the County of Coffee
at the Court house in the town of Manchester the foregoing
last will and testament of David Montgomery Deceased was pro-
P-187 duced in open Court and proven by the oaths of Margaret
Broomfield and Caroline Short, subscribing witnesses thereto
and ordered to be recorded which is accordingly done
    Witness my hand at office this 7th day of December 1846
                J. W. Anderson Clerk
                of the County Court

    I, THOMAS BLAIR of the County of Coffee and State of Tenn-
essee being of sound and disposing mind and memory and calling
to mind the uncertainty of life and the Certainty of Death do
make and publish this my last will and testament hereby revoking and making void all other wills by me at any time made
    1st. I direct that my funeral expenses and all my Just
debts be paid as soon after my death as possible out of any money that I may die possessed of or that may first come into the
hands of my executors
    2nd. I give and bequeath to my beloved wife Eleanor my ne-
groe man Cy about forty years of age, two of the best horses be
longing to me at my death a good saddle and bridle and blanket
two choice cows and calves and two of the best beds and bedstead and furniture as she may wish to keep.
    3rd. I give and bequeath to my son Alexander M Blair, and
my son in law Martin Hancock in trust for the use and benefit
of my Daughter Amanda J. Poindexter and her children the tract
of land whereon she now resides bounded as follows beginning
at a rock the head of the spring thence North 33o 18 poles to
astake and Elm Bush thence North 67o W 76 poles to a white walnut, thence W 94 poles to two hickories on the ridge thence S
14 E 35 poles to a stake and pointers, thence north 81o E 40
poles to a stake, thence South 62o E 20 poles to a stake thence
S 38o E 22 poles to a stake thence South 11o E 22 poles to a
stake and pts thence South 68o E 60 poles to an Elm and Sugar
tree, thence north with Hancock line 20 poles continuing in the
same directions 51 poles to a white walnut on the bluff thence
North 67o W 4 poles to the beginning.
    In addition to the above tract or parcel of land I give
and bequeath to said Blair and Hancock for the use and benefit
of Amanda J. Poindexter one eight day clock and bureau one bed
and bedstead and furniture.
    The above tract of land clock bureau bed and furniture be-
ing of the value of five hundred dollars, the trustees aforesaid
are hereby vested with full power and authority to sell said
land and other property and purchase elsewhere and dispose of
and use in every respect said land and other property in such a
way and manner as shall be by them deemed best calculated to effect the object of such trust, and I hereby enjoin it upon said

trustees at any time they may think the safety of said property
or the interest of the cetin que trust require it to take into
their possession said land and rent or so manage said land and
other property and apply the proceeds in such a manner as may
best promote the interest of my said daughter and her children
during her lifetime and at her death I direct that what may remain of the share above devided to my daughter be equally devided between the heirs of her body or be jointly conveyed to
P-189 them

4th. I direct that the balance of my lands, negroes and
other property be sold and the proceeds thereof be equally divided among my other children (to wit) Cunthia Dillard Mary Hancock A. M. Blair Miriam Farrar Thomas Blair, L. B. Blair Martha
A. Hudson or other heirs of such as may be dead haveing a
child or children living, each of the heirs above named account
ing for money or other property they may have received over and
above a horse saddle bed and furniture and some stock all having had the last named articles of about equal value.

I hereby request and nominate A. Maxwell my executor,

In testimony whereof I have hereunto set my hand and seal
this December 24th in the year of our Lord 1845

Thomas Blair (SEAL)
Chrisley Messick
Saml Hancock

State of Tennessee
Coffee County

At a County Court began and held for the County of Coffee
at the Court house in the town of Manchester on the 4th day of
January 1847 the foregoing will of Thomas Blair deceased was
produced in open Court by the executor therein named and proven
by the oaths of Cristly Messick, and Saml Hancock subscribing
witnesses thereto and orederd to be recorded.

Witness my hand at Office this 5th day of January 1847

J. W. Anderson Clerk

P-190   In the name of God Amen
I, ABNER DUNCAN of the County of Coffee and State of Tennessee
being of sound mind but weak of body do make and publish this
my last will and testament hereby revoking and making void all
former wills by me at any time heretofore made.

And first I direct that my ____ be decently intered in a
manner suitable to my condition in life, and as to such worldly
goods as it has pleased God to intrust me with, I dispose of
the same as follows

1st. I direct that all my debts and funeral expenses be
paid as soon after my decease as possible out of any money that
I may die possessed of or that may first come into the hands of
my executors from any portion of my estate real or personal.

2d. I leave to my beloved wife Anne tha undisturbed possession of the houses and plantation whereon I now reside with
the household and kitchen furniture, with the exception of one

bed and stock as it now stands during her natural life or widowhood.

I also leave to her during the same time Vincy and her
youngest children, that is Martin Cloe & Rosanna with the priv-
<u>alage</u> of keeping Tom as long as she can manage him or until her
death or marriage for the purpose of helping raise her children
but whenever he becomes unmanagable it is my desire she hand
him over to my executor to hire out

3rd. The balance of my negroes with the exception of Creasy and her child, viz. that is David Dick and Jack I desire my
P-191 executor may hire out being particular to have them well
treated

4th. Having had in contemplation for some time to sell
Creasy and her child for the purpose of paying my debts. It is
my desire that my executor sell them for the best price he can
get at private sale, for that purpose Rolley Cunningham is want-
ing to purchase and she being desirous to go then it is my wish
he may get her if he will give as good a price as any one else

5th. I wish the clothes belonging to my former wife and on
one bed, given to my two children by her viz. Catherine and Daniel

6th. I give and bequeath to my wife Anna Duncan my negro
girl Rosanna to despose of as she wishes

7th. It is my wish that my executor out of the proceeds of
the hire of my servants and any other moneys that may come into
his hands belonging to my estate raise and educate my children
in a genteel manner and when they arrive at mature ages to divide the property and money belonging to my estate among my
children equally.

I do hereby constitute and appoint my esteemed neighbor
and friend Thomas Hill executor of this my last will and testament in witness whereof I Abbner Duncan have set my hand and se
seal this 3rd day of January 1847   Abner Duncan (SEAL)
In presence of us   W. R. Brixey
                                    Joseph Gentry
                                    Walton Brixey

State of Tennessee
Coffee County
  At a County Court began and held for the County aforesaid at
the Court house in the town of Manchester on the 1st Monday of
June 1847 this last will and testament of Joseph Gentry was
produced in open Court by the executor therein named and proven
by the oaths of W. L. Brixey and Anthony Clark subscribing witnesses thereto and ordered to be recorded
                                    J. W. Anderson Clerk

                    In the name of God Amen
I, JOSEPH GENTRY of the County of Coffee and State of Tennessee
being weak in body but perfectly sound in mind and believing
from the knowledge I have of my situation I cannot survive this

long I therefore feel the neccessity of amking and publishing
this my last will and testament hereby revoking and making
void all other wills by me at any time heretofore made

1st. I direct that my body be decently intered in said
County in a manner suitable to my situation in life and as to
such worldly estate as it hath pleased God to intrust me with I
dispose of the same as follows.

1st. I direct that all my debts and funeral expenses be
paid as soon after my decease as possible out of any moneys
that I may die possessed of or that may first come into the
hands of my executors form any portion of my estate real or per
sonal

2d. I give and bequeath to my son Hugh one cow one bed
and furniture and all the balance of my property both personal
and real. I give and bequeath to my beloved wife Mary during
her natural life and at her death if she should die before my
unfortunate children to wit, Geo. Nicholas, Sarah, Angeline and
Eliza, I direct that my estate retained in the hands of my executors or so much thereof as will support and keep them from
being chargable so long as they live,

I do hereby make ordain and appoint my beloved sons Jarret
and Hugh executors of this my last will and testament in witness
whereof I Joseph Gentry the said testator have to this my will
written on one sheet of paper set my hand and seal this 7th day
of April in the year of Glrd one thousand eight hundred and forty seven signed sealed and published   Joseph Gentry (SEAL)
in the presence of us who have subscribed in the presence of the
testator and of each   October. Witnesses W. L. Brixey
                                          Thos. J. Harmon
                                          Thos. Hile
                                          Anthony Clay

P-194 I, SARAH NICHOLS do hereby make and publish this my last
will and testament hereby revoking and making void all other
wills by me at any time heretofore made

1st. I give and bequeath to said Cynties Nichols all my
interest in the tract of land on which I now reside I also
give the said Cynthea Nichols a promisayg note under seal dated
the 10th day of December 1844 and due to me one day after date
for twenty nine hundred and nineteen dollars payable to me by
said Cynthia Nichols being the condideration in a part for a
family of negroes sold by me to the said Cynthea Nichol the
names and discription of which negroes will more fully appear
reference being had to the bill of sale made by me of this date.

2nd. I give to Quella James Hall son of William Hall my
bed and furniture

3rd. I give and bequeath to said Cynthis Nichols all my
interest in the estate of my brother Jacob Nichols decd. both
real and personal

Finally, I give and bequeath to the said Cynthia Nichols
all the rest and residue of whatever property real or personal
that I may die possessed of . I also give to her all cases in

action and debts that may be due me in any and every form

Lastly I nominate and appoint the said Cynthia Nichols Executrix of this my last will and testament and hereby request and direct her to undertake the execution of the same given under my hand and seal this 13th day of December 1843

Sarah (X) Nichol (SEAL)

P-195 Signed in the presence of each other this 13th day of June 1845

W. P. Hickerson
Danl. McClean

State of Tennessee
Coffee County

At a County Court bagan and held for Coffee County on the 1st Monday in September 1847 this last will and testament of Sarah Nichols deceased was produced to Court by W. P. Hickerson Attorney at law and proven by the oaths of W. P. Hickerson and Daniel McClean subscribing witnesses thereto and ordered to be recorded

J. W. Anderson Clerk
By James Darnell D. C.

State of Tennessee
Coffee County

At a County Court began and held for the County aforesaid on the 1st Monday of November 1847 this last will and testament of Larkin Ford Sr. Deceased was produced in open Court by M. B. Ford executor and proven by the oaths of Daniel Wiser and William Wiser subscribing witnesses thereto and ordered to be recorded

J. W. Anderson Clerk
By James Darnell D. C.

State of Tennessee
Coffee County

I, LARKIN FORD SENR. being of sound mind and perfect memory do make and publish this my last will and testament manner and form following

1st. I will and bequeath to my son Edmond G Ford all my animal stock and working utensils

2nd. I will and bequeath to my daughter Elizabeth M Ford P-196 one cotton wheel and card and one check real and and one small table and one dinner pot and hooks and one oven and lid

3rd. I will and bequeath to my grand daughter Tabitha Jane Ford daughter of my son M. A. Ford forty six dollars

4th. I will and bequeath to my daughter Jane Crosslean one dollar to be her portion

5th. All table ware household and kitchen furniture which are not herein named I desire to be devided between my son Edmond Ford and my two daughters namely Keziah and Elizabeth as they may think proper

6th. All the right and tittle I have in and to one hundred acres of land lying on the headwaters of Dobbs Creek I desire to be sold to the highest bidder at twelve months credit

Also my bridle and saddle gun, house clock and large chest
to to be sold on a twelve months credit to the highest bidder
and when that and all debts that are then owing to me and all
the moneys I then have is collected and my debts paid I desire
the remaining part to be equally devided among my seven sons
and four daughters namely Matheal A. Mathew B. Simion T. Larkin
S. Stephen H. Thomas S. Edmond G. Patsy Hunt Louisa Ferrell Ki-
ziah and Elizabeth and Jane Crosslins Children and the said
Jane Crosslins Children to have an equal portion then to be appropriated the support of said children and the said Jane Crosslins receipt shall be good
P-197 7th. And lastly it is my desire that my son Edmond G. Ford
should hold possession of all the lands which I have on the head
waters of Noahs fork of Duck River provided he will in a term of
four years after the date of my decease pay four hundred and
fifty dollars to be equally devided among my other six sons and
four daughters and Jane Crosslin children as above directed,but
if Edmond dont choose to hold the land as above described it
shall be sold to the highest bidder payment and to be made in
three equal annuel payment and when collected Edmond shall have
one equal portion as first directed in other moneys and also the
crop then on the ground and shall make his choice in three
months after my decease.
     I hereby appoint Mathew B. Ford Larkin S. Ford and Edmond G
Ford Executors of this my last will and testament hereby revoking and making void all other wills by me made and no claims to
come against any of the children except is found in writing
     In witness whereof I have hereunto set my hand and affixed
my seal this 29th day of June 1847 (six dollars interlined before
assigned)   Larkin Ford (SEAL)
Witnesses   Daniel Wiser
                                       William (X) Wiser
Signed sealed delivered and declared by the above named Larkin
Ford sr. to be his last will and testament in presence of us who
have here subscribed our names as witnesses in the presence of
the testator   Witnesses, Daniel Wisor William Wisor

P-198 State of Tennessee
Coffee County March 1st 1847
     In the name of God Amen knowing that it is appointed for
all men once to die I Johnathon Phillips being in my right mind
do ordain and pablish this my last will and testament
     1st. I will my body to return to its Mother Earth in a de-
cent manner, my soull to God who gave it
     2nd. I give and bequeath to my wife Sarah Phillips the
house and allthe land lying on the South westside of the new
road leading from Manchester to Jasper And one mulatto man
named Lewis, and she is to have choice of all the horses on the
plantation and her saddle and bridle &C. two cows four head of
sheep three sows and pigs and stock hogs sufficient for one
years provision two beds and furniture, two turned cherry beds

steads noe cubbard and small bureau and all the things that
belong to the cubbard, such as plates dishes cups, saucers
pans knives forks and glasses &C. all these things belong to
her during her widowhood if she marries again all goes to the
benefit of my children by her. She is also to have one half
the geese one as two hoes two plows one set of plow gears one
chest and table one wash pot one dinner pot one oven and skil-
let one wheel and cards clock and glass

 3rd. The balance of my estate to be equally devided among
my first children except Giles Richardson I give him one horse
that is all he is to have, that is to say I have already given
P-199 one sorrel horse worth thirty or forty dollars

 4th. I appoint my son William Y Phillips and Hiram Harpool
my executors. Hereby disannulling all other testaments in wills
by me made

 Witness my hand &C. in presence of Michael Stephens W. M.
Roach R. F. Ross   Johnson Phillips

State of Tennessee
Coffee County

 At a County Court began and held for Coffee County on the
1st Monday in January 1848 this last will and testament of
Johnson Phillips deceased was presented in open Court by William Y. Phillips one of the executors and proven by the oaths of
Michael Stephens and Rice F. Ross subscribing witnesses thereto
and ordered to be recorded   J. W. Anderson Clerk
         By James Darnell D. C.

State of Tennessee
Coffee County

 At a County Court began and held for the County aforesaid
on the first Monday of February 1848 this last will and testament of William Lusk Decd. was presented in open Court by James
F. Phillips the executor and proven by the oaths of William
Towery and Elizabeth Robertson subscribing witnesses thereto
and ordered to be recorded. Witness my hand at office this 7th
day of Feby 1848   J. W. Anderson Clk.
         By James Darnell D. C.

P-200 I. WILLIAM LUSK do make and publish this my last will and
testament hereby revoking and making void all other wills by me
at any time made

 1st. I direct that my funeral expenses and all my debts be
paid as soon after my death as possible out of any money that I
may die possessed or may first come into the hands of my executor

 2nd. I give and bequeath to my beloved wife Salley Lusk
the tract of land where I now live all the house hold and kitchen furniture all the money and notes that may be in my possession at my death, two head of horses two cows and calves one
sow and pigs and stock of hogs sufficient to make the second

year after my death, two head of sheep all the poultry and the
first years provision

3rd. I give and bequeath to my beloved Children, Polly Hog-
an James G. Lusk, Joseph Lusk Ruth Phillips and the heirs of my
daughter Elizabeth Becknell as one heir all my estate to be e-
qually devided between them

Lastly I do hereby nominate and appoint James Phillips my
executor In witness whereof I do to this my will set my hand and
seal this 15th day of December 1847   William (X) Lusk (SEAL)
Signed sealed and published in our presence and we having subscribed our names hereto in the presence of the testator this 15
th day of December 1847 Witnesses   William Lowery
                                          Elizabeth (X) Roberson

P-201 State of Tennessee
Coffee County

At a County Court began and held for the County aforesaid
in the town of Manchester on the first Monday of February it
being the 7th day of the month 1848 this last will and testament of Howell Hathcock deceased late of said County was presented in Open Court by Mary Hathcock the executrix therein named and proven by the oaths of John Banks and Alexander Ensey
subscribing witnesses thereto and ordered to be recorded

Witness my hand at Office this 7th day of 1848
                              J. W. Anderson Clerk
                              By James Darnell D. C.

                "In the name of God Amen"
I, HOWELL HATHCOCK of the County of Coffee and State of Tennessee, Farmer being in usual health of body and of sound mind and
disposing memory and calling to mind the uncertainty of this
life and the certainty of death do think it proper to make and
ordain this my last will and testament in the manner and form
following

Item 1st. I give my body to the dust from whence it came
and soul to God who gave it, having strong and unshaken confi-
dence of their reservation of the reserrection morn to dwell
eternally with God and the Angels in Heaven

Item 2nd. I give and bequeath to my beloved wife Mary all
of my household goods and furniture together with all my ef-
ffects debts dues and demands to be at her will and disposal
together with my dwelling house and plantation to live on and
enjoy during her natural life

P-202 Item 3rd. I will and bequeath my tract of land containing two hundred and forty six acres one forth acres to my two
sons Howell J. Hathcock and J H Hathcock the said tract of
land to be divided in the following manner, the dividing to
begin in the centre of the west boundary line of the survey
and running due east until it strike the Kirkland Branch with
its meandering to its Junctions with the Bonner Fork of Duck
River thence down the River to the mouth of the Goose Pond

Branch then up said branch so far as until a due East Cource
with run out of the centre of the East boundary line of said
survey of two hundred and forty six and a fourth acres. I
will to my son Howell P J Hathcock all the land and improvements on the south side of said dividing line, and I allso
will to my son John H Hathcock all the land and improvements
on the north side of said boundary line
        Item 4th. I will and direct that each tract of the above
land be valued and that my beloved and only daughter Queen
√Nashtie Hathcock have one hundred dollars in money to be paid
by my two sons Howell P J Hathcock and John H. Hathcock each
to pay the sum of fifty dollars and when they become of age to
have five years each to pay their respective sums of one hundred dollars to my daughter Queen Nashtie and in the event
that either or any of the legatees should die leaving no lawful heir or heirs then the surviver or survivors to have and
P-203 enjoy the portion or portions of the deceased and should
they all be called off leaving no heirs then my beloved wife
Mary to have all the property at her command to will and dispose of at her pleasure entirely, and to son H. P. J. Hathcock
I give my shot gun when he shall become of age, and to my son
J. N. Hathcock, I give my regle gun when of age, and to my oldest son Miles Hathcock I have already given his part and more
too (to wit) fifty acres of land on which he now lives and other
property which would be over his equal share
        Item 5th. I make appoint and ordain my beloved wife Mary
Hathcock sole executrix of this my last will and testament, ut-
terly revoking all former wills or testament whatever
        In witness whereof I have unto this my last will and test-
ament set my hand and seal the ___ day of ____ in the year of
our Lord eighteen hundred and forty. Howell (X) Hathcock(SEAL)
Signed sealed and delivered in presence of us.
                                Alexander Ensey
                                John Banks

State of Tennessee
Coffee County
        At a County Court began and held for the County aforesaid
in the town of Manchester on the first Monday it being the 7th
day of August 1848 this last will and testament of T. W. Bowen
decd. late of said County was presented in open Court by G. E.
Bowen and proven by the oaths of Renisonn Davidson and William
Norton subscribing witnesses thereto and ordered to be recorded
P-204 Witness my hand at office this 7th day of August 1848
                                James Darnell Clerk

            "In the name of God Amen"
I, F. W. BOWDEN of the County of Coffee and State of Tennessee
being in sound mind and memory but weak in body do make this my
last will and testament
        1st. My soul I humbly resign to God who gave it and my body

to the dust from whence it came

2nd. I do will and bequeath to my brother Guileemus L.
Bowan the land given to me by my father that is one half of the
tract of land on which my mother lives at this time and my entire list of all the stock on the place after paying my Doctors
bill for the love that I have for him and for his attending on
me and attending to my business and waiting on me when sick.

3rd. That I wish the two negroes Daniel and Prisella to
fall back to fathers estate and be devided as fathers will directs his own property to be devided that is equally among the
heirs, I wish Guileemus L. to take care of mother as long as
she lives that is I want him to see to mother and her business
and see that she never suffers

Given under my hand and seal this 20th day of June 1848

F. W. Brown (SEAL)
Renesson Davidson
W. Norton

Attest

P-205

I, ANGELINA MORGAN wife of Harwood Morgan being weak and feeble
of health but sound in mind and being desirous to dispose of my
real and personal estate of my late fathers Hugh Davidson deceased and with the express consent of my said husband do make
and ordain this as my last will and testament never having heretofore make a will.

1st. I will and bequeath upon a final distribution of said
estate after the death of my mother Jane Davidson now living and
who has a life estate therein that three hundred dollars be paid
by my executors to each of my children of my present marriage
viz. Ann Amanda Morgan William Harrison Morgan and Sarah Elizabeth Morgan and if either of my children above named should die
without issue before said final distribution that legacy of such
be paid to the survivors of survivors

2nd. I will and bequeath that my executors pay of the same
fund and at the same time one hundred dollars to each of my
children of my first marriage Edwin Levander Bryan and Emly Jane
Bryan and if either of them should die without issue before said
final distribution that the survivor of them take his or her
legacy and if both of them should die without issue before such
distribution their legacy to go in equal shares to my three
children bfirst named or the survivors of them

3rd. I wil that if my interest in said estate should be
less than Eleven Hundred dollars the legacy named the each of
said legacys be abated in equal portions

4th. I will and bequeath that if my interest in said estate should succeed the legacies herein given that the surplus
or excess shall be equally distributed among my three children
P-206 first above named or the survivor or survivors of them

5th. I appoint my brothers J. Q. and Robt. B. Davidson
Executors of this my last will and desire they carry the same
faithfully into effect

In testimony whereof I have hereunto set my hand and seal

this 9th day of June A. D. 1848
Test

Angeline Morgan (SEAL)
H. L. Davidson
Uriah Sherrill

State of Tennessee
Coffee County
    At a County Court began and held for Coffee County at the
Court house in the town of Manchester on the 1st Monday in October 1848 it being the 2d. day of said month this last will and
testament of Angelina Morgan deceased of said county was produced in open Court by John Q. Davidson one of the executors
therein named and proven by the oaths of H T. Davidson and Uriah
Sherrill the subscribing witnesses thereto and ordered to be
recorded which is accordingly done
    Witness my hand at office this 2d. day of October 1848
                                James Darnell Clerk

State of Tennessee
Coffee County
    At a County Court began and held for the County of Coffee
at the Court house in the town of Manchester on the 1st Monday
in April 1849 it being the 2d. day of said month the last will
P-207 and testament of Shadrick Tribble deceased late of said
County was produced in open Court and was proven by the oaths
of Elestra Reynolda and John Charles subscribing witnesses
thereto and ordered to be recorded which is accordingly done
                                James Darnell Clerk
    I, SHADRICK TRIBBLE of the State of Tennessee and County
of Coffee being this thirteeth day of December eighteen hundred and forty eight, Eighty years of age and being very infirm
and weak in body but of sound mind and memory calling to mind
the mortality of my body and immortality of my never dying soul
and knowing that it is appointed for all mankind once to die and
go Judgement before Almighty God, do hereby make and ordain
this my last will and testament hereby revoking and making void
all other wills or deeds of any discription heretofore made or
executed by me and do here nominate my two trusty friends Stephen Winton and Langston Morton of the State and County above
named to be my executors to this my last will and testament
    It is my will that they or either of them sell at twenty
days notice on twelve months credit with good bond and security
all of my little house hold and kitchen furniture and two young
mares the gray, so soon as John Allison lays by his crop and
makes her fat and further, to collect my notes on hand as they
become due, a schedule of which is attached to this instrument
with a reference for your information but may not be recorded
P-208 with the will.
    It is my desire that the monies so made be equally devided
among all my grand children as they arrive at a proper time to
receive it. My grandson Leanidas son of my son Larkin and
children of Matelda and Minerve my daughters after giving to my

daughter twenty dollars for her own use for neccessities for herself while living, otherwise to go to the devide as above.

I further authorize my said executors as aforesaid to make a deed of conveyance to Edmond Pendleton or his heirs &C. to the land I sold him so soon as he or they shall make the last payment for said land I sold him

In testimony whereof I have hereunto set my hand and seal the day and date above written,

Acknowledged the same before us

Shadrick Tribble
John Charles
Elisha Reynolds

A. B. My burial expenses and Just debts (If any) first paid

S. Tribble

I, ADAM RAYBURN do make and publish this my last will and testament hereby revoking and making void all other wills by me at any time made

In the first place I direct that my funeral expenses and all my other debts be paid out of any money that I may die possessed of or that may first come into the hands of my executors P-209 2nd I desire that all my property remain in the possession of my beloved wife Sarah Rayburn until my children become of age or marry at which time if they desire they can each have a negro and such other property as my executor think can be spared at valueation keeping a record of all distributions thus made so that in a final settlement each child shall receive an equal share of my estate and further I desire that when my youngest child becomes of age thatmy whole estate be devided equally among my children reserving to my aforesaid wife my negro woman Caroline and in case she should die any one of the other women that she may choose together with the legal interest in my land during her life time

Lastly I do hereby nominate and appoint my beloved wife Sarah Rayburn and my son James G Rayburn and A. Maxwell my executrix and executors who are not required to give security but to be qualified as the law requires and to have power to dispose of personal property from time to time as they think advisable keeping an account of sales and expenditures

In witness whereof I do to this my will set my hand and seal this 13th day of August 1849   A. Rayburn (SEAL) signed sealed and published in our presence and we have subscribed our names hereto in the presence of the testator this 13th day of August 1849 Witnesses

W. S. Waterson
J. A. Brantley

P-210
State of Tennessee
Coffee County

At a County Court began and held for Coffee County at the Court house in the town of Manchester on the 3rd day of September 1849 being the first Monday of said month this last will and testament of Adam Rayburn deceased was produced in open Court by A Maxwell and James G Rayburn the executors therein named and proven by the oaths of William S. Waterson and James A

Brantley the subscribing witnesses thereto and ordered to be
recorded which is accordingly done   James Darnell Clk

I, THOMAS LYNN do make and publish this my last will and
testament hereby revoking and making void all other wills by
me at any time made.

1st. I direct that my funeral expenses and all my debts be
paid as soon after my death as possible out of any money that I
may die possessed of or that may first come into the hands of
my executors

2nd. I give and bequeath to my beloved wife Mathilda Lynn
the several tracts of land where I now live containing two hundred acres be the same more or less, bounded on the north by
Jacob Rosimett and Sarah Davis and on the East by Eliza Freeze
and on the south by what is called the grant tract and Andrew
Lynn and on the weat by the Jackson Lynn tract

3rd. She the said Mathilda Lynn have all my stock of horses
cattle hogs and sheep

4th. All my tools household and kitchen furniture

Now my desire is that she the above named Matilda Lynn
shall have all the above named to use or dispose of in any way
she may please during her natural life and after her death what
ever is remaining to be devided, that is Ephraim Franklin to
have one fifth providin__ he comes back and the balance to be
equally devided between Andrew J Franklin and Tabitha Emaline
Franklin and if Ephraim Franklin dont come back the other two
to have what is left

Lastly I do hereby nominate and appoint George Stroud my
executor

I_ witness whereof I do to t his my will set my hand and
seal this 25th day of August 1849   Thomas Lynn (SEAL)
                                      William Holmes
                                      George Roach
                                      W. H. Myers
Signed sealed and published and we have subscribed our names
hereto in the presence of the testator this 25th day of August
1849

State of Tennessee
Coffee County
I, James Darnell Clerk of said Court for Coffee County
certigy that at a County Court began and held for Coffee County
at the Court house in the town of Manchester on the first day
of October 1849 the foregoing last will and testament of Thomas
Lynn deceased was produced to Court and proven by the oaths of
Geo. Roach and W. H. Meyers two of the subscribing witnesses
thereto and ordered to be recorded which is accordingly done
Witness James Darnell Clerk as aforesaid at office this 15th day
of October 1849   James Darnell Clerk
P-212
State of Tennessee

Coffee County

At a County Court began and held for the County of Coffee at the Court house in the town of Manchester on the first Monday it being the fourth day of February 1850. this last will and testament of Andrew Lynn deceased was presented in open court by William Holmes and Daniel Nelson two of the subscribing witnesses thereto and ordered to be recorded

Witness my hand at office this 4th day of February 1850
James Darnell Clerk

I, ANDREW LYNN do make and publish this as my last will and testament hereby revoking and making void all other wills by me at any time made

1st. I direct that my funeral expenses and all my debts be paid as soon after my death as possible out of any money that I may die possessed of or that may first come into the hands of my executors

2nd. I give and bequeath to my wife Isabell Lynn all my house hold and kitchen furniture and the tract of land that I now live on containing one hundred and nineteen acres during her natural life time

3rd. I give and bequeath to my beloved wife all my farming tools and stock of hogs herses cattle and sheep after taking enough out to pay my debts all during her natural lifetime only that my children Thomas H. James Calvin Louisa Jane and Andrew Jackson have equal to what my two oldest sons have had that is Jacob and William Lynn, I wish them to have this much when they become of age or marry

4th. That my wife Isabell Lynn have the ten acres of land that I bought of John O'Neil during her natural life bounded on the North by Matilda Lynn on the East by John Cross and on the west by the above named one hundred and nineteen acre tract.

Lastly I do hereby nominate and appoint William E Lynn my executor

In witness whereof I do to this my will set my hand and seal this 29th day of January 1850   Andrew (X) Lynn
Signed sealed and published in our presence and we subscribed our names hereto in the presence of the testator this 29th day of January 1850   Witnesses   William Holmes
                                                William Smith
                                                Daniel Nelson

I, WILLIAM LORD have thsi day called to mind my worldly substance being weak in body but being strong in mind do make and publish this as my last will and testament hereby revoking and making void all other wills by me at any time made

1st. I direct that my fnueral expenses and all my debts be paid as soon after my death as possible out of any money that I may die possessed of or that may first come into the hands of my executors

P-214 2nd. I give and bequeath to my wife Elizabeth Lord a cer-

tain tract or parcel of land lying in Coffee County Tennessee
in Lords Branch of the Garrison fork of Duck River in District
no 1 and bounded as follows to wit: beginning on a beech
thence north with Gibsons line fifty nine poles to an Elm
thence north west 66 poles to a stake thence west of south 59
poles to a Cherry tree thence south to a Rock Jefferson Easps
North west corner thence Eastwardly with Nev Easps line to his
north corner thence with Gibsons line to the beginning supposed
to be forty acres be the same omre or less to have and to hold
during her widowhood or lifetime and she is to have free access
to any timbers she may need for to keep up her fence and fire-
wood on any portion of my tract of land, also one sorrell mare
and colt and all my present stock of cattle a heiffer and one
sow and pigs and also my household plunder the rents that are
coming to wit
    I want my wife to have a sufficiency to support her and
what stock she has and if there is more than that I want to be
sold and devided equally for the love and affections I have for
my daughters Malissa
    I bequeath to her one heifer and one sow and pigs and the
above described colt she is to have when she becomes of age
    It is my wish that my executors should sell the balance of
P-215 my tract of land except the lot laid off for my wife and
apply the proceeds equally between all my heirs except Jeramiah
B Lord is to have ten dollars extra to make him equal for a
cow that he did not get there is to be discounted fifty five
dollars out of Michells portion of the land for a horse he received
    I do hereby nominate and appoint Chrisly Messick and Jef-
ferson Easp my executors without security or taking our letters
testimentory
    In witness whereof I do to this my last will and testament
set my hand and seal this 28th day of August 1849
                                William M (X) Lord
Signed sealed and selivered in our presence and we have subscribed our names in the presence of the testator this 28th day
of August 1849   William B Gibson
                                Clayburn C Starnes

State of Tennessee
Coffee County
    At a county Court began and held for the County of Coffee at
the Courthouse in the town of Manchester on the 4th day of November 1850 (being the first Monday in said month) the foregoing
last will and testament of William Lord deceased was produced
to the Court and proven by the oaths of William B. Gibson and
Clayburn C. Starnes subscribing witnesses thereto and ordered
to be recorded which is accordingly done
    Witness James Darnell clerk of the County aforesaid at Of-
fice this 5th day of November 1850   James Darnell Clerk
P-216

I, WILLIAM B. WILSON of the County of Coffee and State of Tennessee do make and publish this my last will and testament hereby revoking and making void all other wills by me at any time made, and as to such worldly estate that it hath pleased God to entrust me with I dispose of the same as follows

1st. I direct that all my debts and funeral expenses be paid as soon after my death as possible out of any money that I may die possessed of or may come into the hands of my executrix

2nd. I give andbequeath to my beloved wife Elizabeth Wilson all the property that I am possessed of both personal and real to have and to hold the same her lifetime and at her death to be equally devided between my lawful heirs

I do hereby make ordain and appoint my beloved wife Elizabeth Wilson my executrix of this my last will and testament.

In witness whereof I william B. Wilson the said testator have to this my will written on one sheet of paper set my hand and seal this 26th day of October in the year of our Lord one thousand and eight hundred and fifty   W. B. Wilson (SEAL) signed sealed and published in the presence of us who have subscribed in the presence of the testator and each other
Witnesses   John P Hindman
                                             William Austell

P-217 State of Tennessee
Coffee County

At a County Court began and held for the County of Coffee at the Courthouse in the town of Manchester on the 3rd day of February 1851 being the first Monday in said month the foregoing last will and testament of William B. Wilson deceased was produced to court and proven by the oaths of John P Hindman and William Austell subscribing witnesses thereto and ordered to be recorded which is accourdingly done

Witness James Darnell Clerk of our said Court at office this 3rd day of February 1851   James Darnell Clerk

I, WILLIAM S WATERSON do make and publish this my last will and testament hereby revoking and making void all other wills by me at any time made

1st. I direct that my funeral expenses and all my debts be paid as soon after my death as possible out of any money that I may die possessed of or that may first come into the hands of my executors

2nd. I give and bequeath to my beloved wife Nancy Watterson during her natural life all my lands on the west side of McBrides creek east of the Stage Road up to and including the field in which the barn is situated thence crossing said creek above the old mill running along the devided ridge in a south eastwardly direction to the acadamy branch thence with the branch to the stage read thence with the said road to the corner of the field lying south of the dwelling house thence with

said field in a southernly direction to Thomas Wattersons line
p-218 and thence with his line running in a northernly direction to Thomas Wattersons line and thence with his line running in a northernly direction to the creek thence up said
creek to the beginning including all the dwelling and out houses on said land with all the household and kitchen furniture
and poultry &C. she is also to select for her own use six
milch cows thirty head of sheep, fifty head of stock hogs sows
and pigs also the buggy and the buggy horse and three mules or
horses one wagon and harness and farming utensils sufficient
for the farm and all the oats in the wheat field all the crop
of rye and a sufficient quantity of hay and fodder two hundred
barrels of corn four thousand pounds of pork one or two small
beeves and one winter beef and one hundred dollars in cash she
is also to select three negroes men to cultivate her farm and
two negroe women and boy and one girl

If there is anything set forth above that she does not wish
to be troubled with she may hand it over to the executors

3rd. I give and bequeath to my son William B a tract of
land containing __ acres already deeded to him which he is to
have measured and accounted for at eighteen dollars per acre as
a part of his interest in the estate after deducting one thousand dollars the amount paid the other heirs to make them equal
I also give him my watch

P-219 4th. I give to my son Thomas H a tract of land containing
__ acres already deeded to him which he is to have measured to
him and account for at Eighteen dollars per acre as a part of
his Interest in the estate after deducting one Thousand dollars
the amount paid the other heirs, to make them equal I also give
him my negro boy George to make him equal with the other children who have already received a negro apiece

5th. I give and bequeath to the Cumberland presbyterian
church at Beech Grove five hundred dollars in stock in the N&C
R. R. the interest arising from which is to be appropriated by
my executors for the purpose of sustaining the ministry and o-
ther expenses neccessary to keep said church

6th. I do hereby nominate and appoint Andrew Maxwell and
William B Watterson my executors who are authorized to sell
rent lease or devide any lands I now have or that may hereafter
fall to me. And also to devise or sell the slaves on hand not
otherwise disposed of I wish them also to sell a sufficiency
of my perishable property for cost to pay my debts if neccessary

It is also my will that whatever of my estate may fall to
my son H. M. Watterson be retained in the hands of my executors
be retained until I am released from any and all liabillities
as security or endorser for him

It is also my will that whatever portion may fall to my
daughter Mary Bucannon used to the benefit of all her children
to fare equal and share and share alike

It is also my will that my executor be not required to

give security
In witness whereof I do to this my will set my hand and
P-220 seal this 2nd day of July 1851   William Watterson(SEAL)
Signed sealed and published in our presence and we have sub-
scribed our names hereto in the presence of the testator
Witnesses   J. A. Brantley
                                             B. F. Moore

State of Tennessee
Coffee County
        At a County Court began and held for the County of Coffee
at the Courthouse in the town of Manchester on the 4th day of
August 1851 being the 1st Monday of said month the foregoing
last will and testament of William Watterson deceased was produced to Court and proven by the oaths of James A. Brantley
one of the subscribing witnesses thereto,
        And at a County Court began and held for the County of
Coffee at the Court house in the town of Manchester on the 1st
day of September 1851 the same being thefirst Monday in said
month, the same was proven by the Oath of B. F. Moore the other
subscribing witness thereto and ordered to be recorded which is
according__ done
        Witness my hand at Office this 1st day of September 1851
                                   James Darnell Clerk

                In the name of God Amen
I, JOHN FARRAR of the County of Coffee and State of Tennessee be
ing on the decline of life but sound and perfect of mind and
memory thanks be to God for the same and knowing that it is ap-
P-221 pointed for all people to die, do make and ordain this my
last will and testament
        1st. I commend my soul to Almighty God and my body to be
decently buried and as touching my worldly estate wherewith it
has pleased God to blessme with I give and dispose of it in the
following manner
        After all my Just debts are paid I give and bequeath unto
my beloved wife June Farrar all my land and property debts Judg-
ements and executions and all that belongs to my estate during
her natural life time and after her death I wish all my property
to be equally ___ between all my children
        My beloved son Trollio Farrar heirs Lorenzy Dow Farrar's
heirs by a deduction of Fifty Five dollars off of his part and
Cicero Farrars heirs by a deduction of Fifty Seven dollars of
his part and Malinda Yates and theheirs of her body and thirty
five dollars over my sons part as my sons have had horses
        And my daughter Selina Wileman and the heirs of her body
and Jane Hinkle and the heirs of her body both to have thirty
five dollars apiece in lieu of their beasts and Mary Miles heirs
to have their mothers share together with thirty five dollars
in lieu of a beast and my son John Q. A. Farrar a deduction of

forty six dollars and forty four cents

And my beloved wife shall have the liberty to dispose of her beds and bedclothes as she may think proper

And I hereby appoint my beloved son John Q. A. Farrar P-222 executor of this my last will and testament and I do revoke all wills by me heretofore made and so by these presents acknowledge this to be my last will and testament

John (X) Farrar

Signed Sealed and acknowledged in the presence of us this 21st day of April 1849 Attest

E. A. Rutherford
Thomas Atkinson
Walton Brixey

State of Tennessee
Coffee County

At a County Court began and held for Coffee County at the Courthouse in the town of Manchester on the 6th day of January 1852 the foregoing last will and testament of John Farrar deceased was produced to Court and proven by the oaths and proven by the oaths of Walton Brixey and E. A. Rutherford two of the subscribing witnesses thereto and ordered to be recorded which is accordingly done

Witness my hand this 10th day of January 1852

James Darnell Clerk

In the name of God Amen

I, DAVID HICKERSON do make and publish this my last will and testament hereby revoking all wills by me at any time made

Item 1st. My will is that my bottom Plantation be sold that is beginning at the cross fence between powers and me near the road thence with that up the river to where the Thrower Spring Branch runs into the river thence with that to the spring then in a straight line to where the road leading to Holstenbaker leaves the Road coming from my bottom Plantation to my house then with said Road that leads to Holstenbakers thence with Holstenbakers line, to Mrs. Nancy Hickersons line and with that to Thomas Powers line and with that to the beginning,

2nd. My boy Jim I desire to be hired out at Shelbyville for the year 1852 at the end of that time I desire him to be sold

3rd. The balance of my land household and kitchen furniture hogs cattle sheep and farming utensils and a brown mare, I give to my wife Martha, the land during her life or widowhood and the other property absolutely, the aforesaid land and negroes to be sold by my executors hereinafter named upon a credit the land on a credit of one and two years the negro on a credit of twelve months retaining a lieu on each until the purchase money is collected

I desire my executors to put the same as interest in good homes and to pay over the interest arrising therefrom to my said wife as she may need it

4th. At the death of my wife I desire the aforesaid money
together with the proceeds of the balance of my land hereby
given to my __ during her natural life and which I desire sold
also by my executors at her death

I disire the same to be equally decided between my children and should any of them die their children to take the share
P-224 their deceased parents wuold have been entitled to if
living each one first accounting for what I have heretofore
given them

5th. My saddle horse and such other things as are not herein decreed or my wife may not need, I desire my executors to
sell to pay whatever debts I may owe

6th. I hereby nominate and appoint Charles Hickerson executor of this my last will and testament this 10th day of October 1851   David (X) Hickerson(SEAL)
Signed sealed in our presence by the testator and subscribed
by us in the presence of the testator this 10th October 1851
Witnesses   W. P. Hickerson
                                         L. D. Hickerson

State of Tennessee
Coffee County

At a County Court began and held for Coffee County at the
Court house in the town of Manchester on the 2nd day of February 1852 the foregoing last will and testament of David Hickerson was produced to court and proven by the oaths of W. P. Hickerson and L. D. Hickerson the subscribing witnesses thereto and
ordered to be recorded which is accordingly done

Witness my hand at office this 5th day of February 1852
                                         James Darnell Clk.
P-225
I, SIMION GILLEY do make and publish this my last will and
testament hereby revoking and making void all other wills by me
at any time made

1st. I direct that my funeral expenses and all my debts be
paid as soon after my death as possible out of any money that I
may die possessed of or that may first come into the hands of
my executors

2nd. I give and bequeath unto my beloved wife Sarah Gilley
to have all my personal property and real estate for the use of
raising the children, then devided equally among them

I do hereby nominate and appoint John Byrom my executor

I_ witness whereof I do to this my last will and testament
set my hand and seal this 12th day of September 1851
                                         Simeon Gilley
Signed sealed and published in our presence and we have subscribed our names hereto in the presence of the testator this
12th day of Sept. 1851 Witnesses   J. W. Whittmore
                                     N. Jernigan

State of Tennessee
Coffee County

At a County Court began and held for Coffee County at the Court house in the town of Manchester on the 2nd day of February 1852 the foregoing last will and testament of Simeon Gilley deceased was produced to Court and proven by the oaths J. W. Whittmore and N Jernigan the subscribing witnesses thereto and ordered to be recorded which is accordingly done

Witness my hand at Office this 5th day of February 1852

James Darnell Clk

P-226
State of Tennessee
Coffee County

I, JAMES McCULLOUGH do make and publish this my last will and testament hereby revoking and making void all other wills by me at any time amde

1st. I direct thatmy funeral expenses and all my debts be paid as soon after my death as possible out of any money that I may die possessed of or that may first come into the hands of my executors

2nd. I give and bequeath to my wife Rhoda McCullough all my corn and pork hogs and all that is in the house and one small colt and one mans saddle and at her death all the above named articles left to belong to James R McCullough Also the said James R McCullough is to have one hundred dollars over an equal share of the rest of my heirs out of the proceeds of my land when sold

I wish my land all rented so long as my wife Rhoda McCullough lives and Richard Robin to have the benefit of the rent by supporting her as long as she lives and taking care of her

And at her death I wish my land all to be sold and equally devided between all my heirs except the above James N McCullough who is to have one hundred dollars over.

I want one bay horse I have sold to pay my debts and to the benefit of my wife

I do hereby nominate my friend Gilbert B. Messick my executor In witness whereof I do to this my last will and testament set my hand and seal this 25th day of December 1851

James (X) McCullough

P-227 Signed Sealed and published in our presence and we have subscribed our names hereto in the presence of the testator the day and date above written Witnesses J. H. Lawerence
Jesse Jernigan

State of Tennessee
Coffee County

At a County Court began and held for Coffee County at the Courthouse in the town of Manchester on the 2nd day of February 1852 the foregoing last will and testament of James McCullough deceased was produced to Court and proven by the oaths of J. H. Lawrance one of the subscribing witnesses thereto and or-

dered to be recorded which is accordingly done
Witness my hand at Office this 5th day of February 1852
James Darnell Clk

I, CHARLES MOORE of the County of Coffee and State of
Tennessee being weak of body but sound of mind and disposing
memory, do make and ordain this my last will and testament in
manner and form following to wit:
1st. It is my will and desire that my executors pay my funeral expenses and all my just debts out of any money that may
be on hand at the time of my death or of the first money that
may be collected from the sale of my property:
2nd. I give and bequeath to my beloved wife Mary Moore
during her natural life my land on which I reside five negroes
(to wit) Charles Mariah Manuel Matty and her child Ann and
their future increase two choice horses three feather bed
steads and furniture four cows and calves my ozen and cart all
my property a years provision one hundred dollars in money my
table chairs bureau cupboard kitchen furniture and twenty
choice stock hogs
3rd. I give to my daughter Sarah F Shanklin during her
natural life and then to her children a negro girl named Rachael and her future increase said negro to be valued to her by
disinterested men in part her portion ofmy estate and which is
not to be subject to the payment of her husbands debts and
should a share amount to more than the value of said negro the
amount above that to be placed in the hands of trustee and for
her to draw annually the interest thereon to use and at my
wife's death that the share of my daughter Sarah F Shanklin,
be placed also in the handsof trustee and for to draw annually
the interest to wit
4th. I will and desire that the balance of my negroes not
named above be valued by disinterested men and put into lots
and drawn for and devided as follows to wit: That William
Moore and Benjamin Moore Sophia Finch Jane Scrugs Susan Hoover
and Eliza Thomas each draw a share to make them equal to Sarah
F Shanklin and that the two children of my son Robert Moore deceased draw only a half share between them and that Martha A.
Moore deceased draw a half share
P-229 5th. I will and desire that the balance of my property
not heretofore named that may be on hand at the time of my
death be sold to the highest bidder on a twelve month credit
and the proceeds devided as above named (ie) that those named
to draw full shares draw them, and those named to draw half
shares draw them also
6th. At the death of my wife I will that the negroes she
may have be valued and devided as above specified and the lands
stock crop &C. be sold on the same terms as above mentioned
and the proceeds devided as before named (ie) that William
Moore Benjamin Moore Sophia Finch Jane Scruggs Susan Hoover Sarah F Shanklin and Eliza Thomas each draw a full share and that

the two children ofmy son Robert Moore deceased draw only a
half share between them and that Martha A Moore daughter of
Martha Moore deceased draw a half share

7th. I appoint my son Benjamin Moore guardian of Martha A.
Moore and if she should die before she marries or becomes of
age that her portion Shall return as a part of my estate and be
devided among my other heirs as above specified

8th. I appoint John E Scruggs and Benjamin Moore executors
of this my last will and testament revoking all other swills by
me made

In witness whereof I have hereunto set my hand and seal
this 31st Decr 1850   Charles (X) Moore (SEAL)
Attesta   G. G. Osborne
                                             A. Maxwell

P-231 State of Tennessee
Coffee County

At a County Court began and held for Coffee County at the
Court house in the town of Manchester on the 1st Monday in June
1852 the foregoing last will and testament of Charles Moore deceased was produced to Court by J. E. Scruggs and Benjamin
Moores the executors therein named and pronen by the oaths of
G G Osborne and A. Maxwell the subscribing witnesses thereto and
ordered to be recorded which is accordingly done

Witness my hand at Office this 8th day of June 1852
                                             H. M. Short   Clerk

I, MARY TILLMON do make and publish this as my last will
and testament hereby revoking and making void all other wills
by me at any time made

1st. I direct that my funeral expenses and all my debts be
paid as soon after my death as possible out of any money that I
may die possessed of or that may first come into the hands of
my executors

2nd. I give and bequeath to my daughter Tildy Tillmon forty acres of land to her and her bodily heirs to be taken off the
north end of the land adjoining A Freeman and D. Nelson and also one oven and one Coffee mill

3rd. I give and bequeath to my daughter Polly Smith forty
acres of land adgoining Julians forty acres to include the im-
P-231 provements to her and her bodily heirs and one little ket-
tle

4th. I have given to my daughter Julian and her bodily
heirs her portion of land to wit forty acres to come to the
Spring Branch and I give her my largest pot one tub and setting
chair and sifter

5th. I give to my daughter Jane Beals three children and
Hannah Gunns four children the balance of the land where I live
after the other three girls get their forty acres each and then
these children to have the hundred acres that lies in Cannon
County all that to be sold and the money arrising from it to be

equally devided among those seven children

6th. I leave my cow and calf to be sold and the money devided between my five daughters children

7th. I leave the balance of my little stuff in the house
to Tildy Tillmon and Polly Smith and fort hem to get two disinterested women to devide it between them equally without any
grumbling

In witness whereof I do to this my last will and testament set my hand and seal this 21st day of August 1849

Mary (X) Tillmon (SEAL)

Signed sealed and published in our presence and we have subscribed our names hereto in the presence of the testator
Witnesses   John Brandon Jonathon
                                       Jonathan G. Davis
N. B. I do appoint Tildy Tillmon my executrix to this my last
will and testament.

State of Tennessee
Coffee County
P-232 At a County Court began and held for Coffee County at the
Court house in the town of Manchester on the 5th day of July
1852 the foregoing last will and testament of Mary Tillmon deceased was produced to Court and proven by the oaths of Jonathan G Davis one of the subscribing witnesses thereto and ordered to be recorded which is accordingly done

Witness my hand at Office this 5th day of July 1852

A. M. Short Clk

I, SMITH BLANTON being of sound mind and desposing memory
but feeble in body do make and publish this my last will and
testament

1st. I will and desire that my funeral expenses as well as
all my Just debts be paid as soon as possible after my death
out of any money that I may die sized and possessed of

2nd. After all my debts shall have been paid I will and bequeath all the residue of my property of every kind and discription to my wife Nancy for her sole use and desposition

3rd. It is further my will and desire that my executors
whom I hereinafter appoint may be permitted to execute this my
will without entering into bond and security and that they proceed to execution thereof by disposing of any of my property
that they may deem neccessary either at public or private sale
for the satisfaction of my Just and lawful debts

4th. I do hereby constitute and appoint my wife Nancy my
executrix and my brother Willis Blanton my executor to this my
last will and testament

In testimony whereof I hereunto set my hand and seal this
12th day of August 1852   Smith Blanton (SEAL)
Signed in our presence this 12th August 1852
Attest   P. H. Price   John G. Willis

State of Tennessee
Coffee County

At a County Court began and held for Coffee County at the Courthouse in the town of Manchester on the 6th day of September 1852 the foregoing last will and testament of Smith Blanton deceased was produced to Court by the executrix and executor therein named and proven by the oaths of John G. Willis one of the subscribing witnesses thereto and ordered to be recorded which is accordingly done

Witness my hand at Office this 16th day of September 1852

A. M. Short   Clerk

April 21st 1852

This will does away with all other wills this is my last will and testament

I will my wife after paying all my funeral expenses and all debts that I may owe, which money to be paid out of the first money coming to the hands of my administrator and then my wife to have Peter and Clark and Matilda three negroes two boys and one girl and the tract of land that I live on and the tract of P-234 land that I bought of John Eoff the two tracts to contain three hundred and two acres and the smith tools and as much stock of every kind as she may need for her use and one years provision and the household and kitchen furniture laid off for her use during her life and at her death my son Robert C Carden lives with her is to have the three hundred and two acres that are above mentioned and a negroe boy named Peter and a girl named Martha which I bought of the two Nortons and Harris and all the property his mother has except Clark and Matilda two negroes William L. Carden to have a negro boy named Jerry and Martin A Carden to have a nebroe boy called Clark and Lucinda J Jackson and Robert C Carden at my death

I_ witness whereof I have set my hand and seal this 21st day of April 1852   Reuben Carden   (SEAL)
In the presence of us   Robt. McGuire
                                         Eliza J McGuire

State of Tennessee
Coffee County

At a County Court began and held for Coffee County at the Court house in the town of Manchester on the 4th day of October 1852 the foregoing last will and testament of Reuben Carden deceased was produced to Court and proven by the oath of Robt. Mc Guire one of the Subscribing witnesses thereto and ordered to be recorded which is accordingly done

Witness my hand at Office this 6th day of October 1852

A. M. Short   Clerk

I, ANDREW J. FRANKLIN do make and publish this my last will and testament hereby revoking and making void all other wills by me at any time made

1st. I direct that my funeral expenses and all my debts be paid as soon after my death as possible out of any money that I may die possessed of or that may first come into the hands of my executors

2nd. I give and bequeath to Pamelia Franklin my wife one Cart and Steers House hold and kitchen furniture also all the effects that are coming to me by Thomas Lynns will

I do hereby nominate and appoint William Earles my executor

In witness whereof I do to this my will set my hand and seal this 24th day of June 1851   Andrew J. Franklin
Attest   N Jernigan
                                     Martin H Earles

P-236
State of Tennessee
Coffee County

At a County Court began and held for Coffee County at the Court house in the town of Manchester on the 7th day of March 1853 being the first Monday in said month the foregoing last will and testament of Andrew J. Franklin deceased was produced to Court and proven by the oaths of N. Jernigan and Martin H. Earles the subscribing witnesses thereto and ordered to be recorded which is accordingly done

Witness my hand at Office as clerk of said Court this 8th day of March 1853   A. M. Short   Clerk

I, CHARLOTTE S. THOMPSON do make and publish this my last will and testament hereby revoking and making void all other wills by me at any time made

1st. I direct that all my funeral expenses and all my debts be paid as soon after my death as possible out of any money that I may die possessed of or that may first come into the hands of my executors

2nd. I give and bequeath to my son Burwell J Thompson one negor man named Henry aged about thirty five one negro boy named Henry aged about thirty five one negroe boy named John six or seven years old one negro girl named Amanda Seven years old and all other property that I may die seized and possessed of

3rd. I give and bequeath to my Grand daughter Jane B Maupin twenty five dollars to be paid to her by my executors or executor when she becomes twenty one years old

Lastly I do hereby nominate and appoint Burwell J Thompson and Isaac M. Wilkinson my executors

In witness whereof I do to this my last will and testament set my hand and seal this 17th day of May 1853
                           Charlotte S Thompson(SEAL
Signed sealed and published in our presence and we have subscribed our names hereto in the presence of the testator this 17th day of May 1853   Witnesses   R. R. Price
                                      F. F. Price

State of Tennessee
Coffee County

At a County Court began and held for Coffee County at the
Court house in the town of Manchester on the 6th day of June
1853 the foregoing last will and testament of Charlotte S Thompson deceased was produced to Court by Isaac M. Wilkinson and
Burwell J Thompson the executor therein named and proven by the
oaths of R. R. Price one of the subscribing witnesses thereto
and ordered to be recorded which is accordingly done

Witness my hand at Office this 17th day of June 1853

A. M. Short   Clerk

P-238

I, JOHN L. PEAY do make and publish this my last will and
testament hereby revoking and making void all other wills by me
at any time made

1st. It is my will that all my funeral expenses and all my
Just debts be paid as soon after my death as possible out of
any money I may die possessed of or that may first come into the
hands of my executors

2nd. I give and bequeath to my beloved wife Ranny all my
property both real and personal during her natural life or widow
hood

And lastly I do hereby nominate and appoint James Gibson my
executor

In witness whereof I do to this my last will and testament
set my hand and affix my seal this 2nd day of November A. D.
1853   J. L. Peay   (SEAL)

Executed signed and sealed in our presence the day and date
above written   William Ashley
                                  William Keele

State of Tennessee
Coffee County

At a County Court began and held for Coffee County at the
Court house in the town of Manchester on the 7th day of November
1853 (being the first Monday in said month) the last will and
testament of John L Peay deceased was produced to Court by the
executor therein named and proven by the oaths of the subscribing witnesses thereto and ordered to be recorded which is accordingly done

P-239 Witness A. M. Short Clerk of said Court at Office this 9th
day of November 1853   A. M.   Short   Clerk

I, JAMES GREEN of the County of Coffee and state of Tennessee being of sound mind and memory and at the present enjoying
good health but knowing the uncertainty of time allotted to man
and having been permitted to live little better than fifty years
and having been blessed with a large family of children as well
as with a portion of worldly goods and also knowing that the law
of my county makes equitable distribution of intestate estates
but to save my heirs the trouble as well as the expense

I do therefore this 17th day of September eighteen hundred and
fifty make and publish this my last will and testament to wit

In the first place I desire my body to be buried in a decent manner wherever my family may think proper after my decease
It is also my desire that my just debts and funeral expenses be
speedily and puctually paid and what worldly goods I may die
possessed of I desire disposed of in the following manner to wit

To my loving wife and companion Mary Green I will and bequeath all my property both real and personal together with
what ready money I may have at my death to dispose of in the
following manner in the first place to make our surviving children equal to those that have married and left us at the time
when they arrive at lawful age or marry and having made all eque
al say to each one hundred and seventy nine dollare and as near
P-240 the like kind of property which is set out in a book I
keep for that purpose (If not in property then in money)

And should my wife aforesaid live to see our youngest child
of lawful age then I desire her to sell my old tract together
with my entry containing in all one hundred and forty acres in
one lot and also my tract purchased from father including seventeen acres purchased of brother Elijah Green making one hundred
and nineteen acres in one lot sold one two and three years credit, taking bonds with good security for the purchase money also
retaining a lieu on the land until the purchase money is fully
paid and and at the same time to dispose of all the personal
property that she may not want or need on such times as she
thinks best after having made all the children equal as before
stated

I desire the proceeds of the sale before stated equally divided among all of our children if living if not their children
respectively to secure their parents part except my daughter Matilda Moss and her part I desire her part kept specially for her
benefit, if circumstances may require it used for sustanance of
her children if not I desire it kept at interest for the benefit
of her children when and the time of their arriving at age never
and at no circumstances to be placed in the hands of her husband
David Moss nor to be used either directly or indirectly for his
P-241 use or benefit

I do further will and desire that after the death of my
wife my executor will proceed to dispose of my remaining lands
together will all the property remaining, on the terms above directed and devide the proceeds the same as above directed.

And provided my wife does not live to make the disposition
of my property as above directed then I desire my executors at
her death to act and proceed under the same direction given a-
bove, doing equal justice to all and in the manner above specified

Having disposed and directed the disposition of all my
worldly goods, I do now constitute and appoint my sons John
Mitchell Green and William Martin Green my executors and I desire my son John Mitchell to become the guardian of his borther

Willis Henderson Green and provide for him and take charge of
his part of my estate after or before his mothers death,

Also I desire Willis Henderson to live with his mother
during her lifetime

Also I request David R Vance to assist my two sons in the
discharge of their duties as executors

In witness whereof I hereunto sign my name and affix my
seal the day and date above written   James Green (SEAL)
Attest   Willis Blanton
                                            Robt H Green

Codicil

I, JAMES GREEN doth make and publish this my first codicil
to my will as set out in the following language to wit:
P-242 I desire that when the sale takes place as directed in my
will of the lands therein specified that the lands purchased of
my father the sale must not include any land on the north side
of the ridge, in other words, I reserve and attach a small slip
say 4 acres of said tract of land to the tract I now live on all
of which is now under fense

And further since making and publishing my will as aforesaid my son John M Green hath departed this life I do therefore
appoint David R Vance my executor with my son William Martin
Green and desire them to qualify as such

Given under my hand and seal this 28th day of October 1853
                                            James Green (SEAL)
Attest   Willis Blanton
                                            Robert Green

State of Tennessee
Coffee County

At a County Court began and held for Coffee County at the
Court house in the town of Manchester on the 5th day of December 1853 the foregoing will &C. was produced to Court and proven
by the oaths of Willis Blanton and P. H. Green the subscribing
Witnesses thereto and ordered to be recorded which is accordingly done

Witness my hand at Office this 6th December 1853
                                            Hiram S. Emerson Clk
P -243

I, DANIEL H. COUL of the County of Coffee and State of Tenn
essee being of sound mind and memory do hereby make and publish
this as my last will and testament hereby revoking and making
void all former wills by me made

Item, 1st. I will that all my just debts be paid

Item 2nd. I give and bequeath to my beloved wife Nancy all
my plantation upon which I now live with all the buildings and
appertanances thereto belonging with the rents and profits
thereof for and during her natural life

Item 3rd. I also give my beloved wife Nancy any two of my
horses or mares that she may select with a waggon and one yoke
of oxen 4 cows and calves of her own choosing 20 head of hogs
to be selected by herself out of my stock 10 head of sheep

which are also to be chosen by herself

Item 4th. I also give my beloved wife Nancy all my house
hold and kitchen furniture with the farming tools and so much
thereof as she may choose to keep also all the poultry of every
kind

Item 5th. I give and bequeath to my son Caleb Coul two hundred and seventy five dollars in stock in the Nashville and
Chattanooga Rail Road with all the interest or dividends now
that may arrise from the same over and above what he has already had which was a horse and saddle worth eighty dollars one
bed and furniture and eight head of Cattle worth forty dollars
already had

Item 6th I have already given to my son E A Coul one horse
P-244 and saddle worth seventy dollars and four hundred dollars
in land by value estimated

Item 7th. I have already given to my son James H Coul one
horse and saddle worth seventy dollars and four hundred dollars
in land by value estimated

Item 8th. I have given to my daughter Martha J Clayborne
one cow and calf and one bed and furniture and one dressing table all worth thirty five doolars and four hundred dollars in
land by value estimated

Item 9th. I give to my son H. H. Coul one horse and saddle
and one hundred acres in land worth five hundred dollars in value as specified in a deed to him by me made already

Item 10th. I give to my son Andrew J Coul one horse and saddle and at the death of his mother one hundred and seventeen
acres of land on which I now live which is bounded as follows
to wit

Beginning at a bunch of Elder bushes in the west branch of
Bradley Creek in George Millers South boundary line and running
west with his line four hundred poles to a stake said Millers
S. W. Corner thence south 53 poles to a stake and chestnut and
oak pointers thence east 160 poles to a stake thence north 8
poles to opposite the end of a cross fence 164 poles to a stake
thence south 42o east five poles to two bushes at the head of t
the big springs thence down the spring branch to Bradly's Creek
and up the Creek with its meanderings to the beginning

Item 11th. I give and bequeath to my daughter Manda A Coul
one hundred and twelve acres of land lying Joining James H Couls
land and the above discribed tract and bounded as follows to
wit beginning on the black oak James H. Coul N. E. Corner and
running south 89½o west 287½ poles to a stake, said James H.
Coul N. W. Corner thence N 53 poles to a stake and chestnut
pointers A. J. Coul S. W. Corner thence east with the south
boundary line of his land to the big spring and down the same
and the meanders of Bradly Creek to the beginning

But the above tracts of land are to belong to my wife so
long as she lives as recited in the 2nd Item of this will

Lastly I hereby nominate and appoint Elconer A. Coul and
James H. Coul my sons my executors of this my last will and

testament
In testimony whereof I have hereunto set my hand and affix
my seal this 22nd day of May A. D. 1852 Daniel H. Coul (SEAL)
Signed sealed and acknowledged and declarred by the testator to
be his last will and testament in our presence
                                        I. T. Roberts
                                        I. C. Wildman

State of Tennessee
Coffee County
     At a County Court began and held for Coffee County at the
Court house in the town of Manchester on the 2nd day of January
1854 being the first Monday in said month the foregoing last
P-246 will and testament of Daniel H Coll was produced to Court
by Eleanor A Coul and James H Coll the executors therein named
and proven by the oaths of I. T. Roberts and I. C. Willman the
subscribing witnesses thereto and ordered to be recorded which
is accordingly done witness my hand at Office this 2nd day of
January 1854   Hiram S. Emerson Clerk

State of Tennessee Coffee County
     I, ELIZAH SUGGS of the County of Coffee and State of Tenn-
essee being afflicted in great bodily debility though of sound
mind and memory do make and constitute this my last will and t
testament
     1st. I give my soul to God from whom I received it, hoping
he will take it in his everlasting rest that he has in reservation for his people
     2nd. I give my body to my friends that they may bury it
decently and it is my request that my funeral expenses first be
paid out of my estate and when this shall have been done it is
my will and wish that all my remaining portion of my estate of
every order should be disposed in the following manner to wit:
     1st. that all my just and legal debts be first paid
     2nd. It is my will and wish that my brother Franklin Sugg
and my sister Lavena Sugg take into the care and immediate possession at my departure all my real and personal estate and effects of every order and description upon the condition that
they do decently support father and mother whilst they may live
in this world and if it is the will of God to take my father
and mother away from the world fist fisst before my brother
Franklen Sugg and Levvena thatthey do still hold possession to
their own proper use and behoof they and their legal offspring
all my real and personal of every discription to be equally devided between them except my reilroad stock in the McMinnville
and Manchester Road, that I give and bequeath to my brother
Franklin Sugg to have for his own suppprt and benefit
     These expression_ above stated constitute my closing wishes
so far as my will is known to myself
     Given under my hand and my seal this 1st day of April in
the year of our Lord 1854   Eliajh Sugg (SEAL)

83.

State of Tennessee
Coffee County
     At a County Court began and held for Coffee County at the
Courthouse in the town of Manchester on the 3rd day of July
1854 the foregoing last will and testament of Elijah Sugg deceased was this day produced to Court and proven by the oaths o
of L. W. Marbery and Simpson Sewell the subscribing witnesses
theto and ordered to be recorded which is accordingly done
     Witness my hand as Clerk of said Court at Office this 3rd
day of July 1854   Hiram S. Emerson (SEAL)

P-248 I, JOHN WILSON do make and publish this as my last will
and testament hereby revoking and making void all other wills
by me at any time made
     1st. I direct that my funeral expenses and all my debts be
paid as soon as possible after my death out of any money that I
may die possessed of or that may first come into the hands of
my executrix
     2nd. I give and bequeath to my sister Jane C. Wilson the
land I now live on for her support her lifetime and also my negro woman Mary and one of her children namely John Beel during
her lifetime and also all the house hold and kitchen furniture
except what will be named hereafter also all of my farming
tools also one gray mare and two choice cows and calves and all
of my farming tools also one gray mare and two choice cows and
calves and all my hogs and sheep and all the bacon and land &C.
and corn and fodder
     3rd. I give and bequeath to my heice Francis Tate one ne-
gro girl named Phebe to her and the heirs of her body also one
bed and furniture
     4th. I wish my bay horse to be sold and saddle and bench
tools and the balance of my cattle
     5th. and last I do hereby constitute and appoint my sister
Jane C Wilson Executrix
P-249 In witness whereof I do to this my will set my hand and
seal this 29th day of April 1854   John Wilson   (SEAL)
Attest   Abner Bryan
                                      V. P. Howard

State of Tennessee
Coffee County
     At a County Court began and held for the County of Coffee
at the Court house in the town of Manchester on the 7th day of
August 1854 the foregoing last will and testament of John Wilson deceased was produced to Court and proven by the oath of
Abner Bryan and J. P. Howard the subscribing witnesses thereto
and ordered to be recorded which is accordingly done
     Witness my hand at Office this 8th day of August 1854
                                      Hiram S. Emerson Clerk

     Nuncupatives of JANE FARRAR, ELIZABETH WALKER and DORCAS
HOWARD being duly sworn depose and say that they were at the

house of Jane Farrar deceased a few days before her death the
precise number of days not <u>recolected</u> said decedent called to
them and said she was very sick and hardly thought she would
ever get up again, and after her death she said she wanted her
three children John Q. A. Farrar Malinda Yates andSelina Wileman to have her beds and bed clothes to be equally <u>de</u>vided between them except the quilts that she had made and she wanted
them given to her grand daughter Eliza Jane Hinkle
    She also said witnesses to see such articles above men-
tioned <u>de</u>vided between the above persons.
P-250 The conversation was at the house of the deceased and <u>ace</u>
<u>cured</u> during her last sickness
Sworn to and subscribed in open Court this 7th day of August
1854   Elizabeth (X) Walker   Darcas (X) Howard
        Hiram S. Emerson Clerk
Proof that Mrs. Farrar died between the 5th & 10th day of July
1854
State of Tennessee
Coffee County
    At a County Court began and held for Coffee County at the
Courthouse in the town of Manchester on the 7th day of August
1854 the foregoing Noncupative will of Jane Farrar deceased
was produced in Court and proven in Open Court by Elizabeth
Walker and Darcas Howard and ordered to be recorded which is
accordingly done
    Witnessmy hand at Office this 8th day of August 1854
        Hiram S. Emerson Clerk

        In the name of God Amen
I, WILLIAM CUNNINGHAM a citizen of Coffee County and State of
Tennessee do hereby make andpublish this my last will and testament that is to say first as I am desirous in making provisions for my wife I do hereby give and bequeath to her during
her life or widowhood all of lands and negroes and all other
property of every species that I may possess together with all
notes monies &C. including every thing that I may possess.
Should she marry then one share only and after her death or
marriage, then I give one share to my son James M Cunningham
and I give one share to John T Cunningham and I give unto my
daughter Elizabeth Ann Cunningham one share to her sole and
seperate use and should she marry to have it entirely free from
her husbands and under her own control and I give one share to
my daughter Virginia Caroline Cunningham one share to her sole
use and benefit in case she should marry to have it entirely
free from her husbands control and under her own and I give to
my daughter Mary L. Cunningham one share to her sole and seperate use in case she should marry to have it entirely free from
her husband andunder her own control
    Now if any of my children should marry and my wife should
make any advancements she is to take account of such advancements so to make them all equal on the day that the <u>de</u>vision

may be <u>maid</u> the true interest and meaning of the first clause
is for the estate not to be wasted but to have the use and benefit during her lifetime or widowhood of all my estate after
her paying all my Just debts

The remainder then to be de̲vided among my children. I
wish them to select each of them or their representatives some
good disinterested persons to make the de̲visions and should any
one get more than another then in that case he is to pay back
so as to make them equally all the estate that my daughters are
entitled under this will should they die then their interest if
there are no bodily heirs to inherit the estate of theirs then
it is to be de̲vided among my surviving children or their children provided their should be any minors. William Cunningham
P-252   (SEAL)
Signed sealed in the presence of us
Witnesses   Samuel McBee
                                         James M Cunningham
Here I add more to the above will that is if my wife hs
should increase the family which I expect she will then and in
that case to share as above Stated, if a daughter to have to
her sole and seperate use should any of my sons or daughters
die and leave no heirs that are lawful then in that case the
estate that they ingerit by birth right shall return to the
rest of my surviving children and their heirs this 2nd day of
November 1853   William Cunningham

State of Tennessee
Coffee County
At a County Court began and held for Coffee County at the
Court house in the town of Manchester on the 2nd day of October
1854 the foregoing last will and testament of William Cunningham deceased was produced to Court and proven in open Court by
James M Cunningham and W. W. Harris and J. T. Crocket as to the
handwriting of the testator the other subscribing witnesses being a non resident of this State and ordered to be recorded
which is accordingly done.
Witness my hand at Office this 4th day of October 1854
                                 Hiram S. Emerson Clerk

P-253 State of Tennessee Coffee County Sept 9th 1854
I, RACHAEL STEPHENS do make and publish this my last will
and testament hereby revoking and making void all other wills
by me at any time made
1st. I direct that my funeral expenses and all my Just
debts be paid as soon after my death as possible out of any
money that I may die possessed of or that may first come into
the hands of my executors
2nd. I give and bequeath that all my personal and Real
Estate be sold and after all my debts be paid and my Mother to
be supported out of the balance so long as she may live and it
has pleased Almighty God to remember

I want the remainder if any to be devided with sister Sarah
and Alison and Lilburn my two brothers and sisters equally
4th. And Lastly to the end and them conclude lastly conclude
I do hereby nominate and appoint John Anthony my executor
In witness whereof I do to this my will set my hand and
seal this 10th day of September 1854   Rachael (X) Stephens(SEAL)
Signed sealed and published in our presence and we have subscribed our names hereto in the presence of the testator this 10th
day of September 1854. Witnesses   A. W. Carroll
                                        William Carroll

State of Tennessee
Coffee County
        At a County Court began and her for Coffee County at the
P-254 Court house in the town of Manchester on the 6th day of
November 1854 the foregoing last will and testament of Rachael
Stephens was produced to Court and proven by the oaths of Jos-
eph S Gray and William Carroll two of the subscribing witnesses
thereto and ordered to be recorded which is accordingly done
this 10th day of November 1854   Hiram S Emerson Clerk

        We,Wm B. Gibson and L. M. Robinson do state that the non-
cupative will of Charles Hickerson was made by him on the 24th
day or October 1854 in our presence to which we were specially
required to beqr witness by the testator himself in the presence of each other that it was made in his last sickness in his
own habitation or dwelling house and the same is as follows
(to wit)
        That after his debts should be paid whatever might be left
of his estate if not more than one dollar that his sister Eliza
Hickerson shall be one of his heirs he also wanted Wm. P. Hickerson and Wiley Hickerson to raise her children
        Made out and signed by us this 6th day of November 1854
                                        Wm. B. Gibson (SEAL)
                                        L. M. Robinson (SEAL)

State of Tennessee
Coffee County
        At a County Court began and held for Coffee County at the
Court house in the town of Manchester on the 6th day of Novem-
ber 1854 (being the first Monday in said month) the foregoing
Nuncupative will of Charles Hickerson deceased was produced to
Court and proven by the oaths of Wm. B. Gibson and L. M. Robin-
son whose names are subscribed to the same, and ordered to be
recorded which is accordingly done
        Witness my hand at Office this 10th day of November 1854
                                        Hiram S. Emerson Clerk

            In the name of God Amen
I, SARAH HOWARD of the County of Coffee and State of Tennessee
being on the decline of life but of sound and proper mind and

memory thanks be to God for the same and knowing that It is appointed for all people to die, do make and ordain this my last will and testament

1st. I Recommend my soul to God and my body to be decently buried and as touching my worldly estate wherewith it hath pleased God to bless me with

1st. I give and bequeath unto my son John P. Howard and his heirs two hundred dollars on account of the deficiency of his tract or lot of land also the crop that was made or on hand except a sufficient quantity of it to do the stock until they are otherwise disposed of

2nd. I give and bequeath to my son James Howard and his heirs two hundred dollars on account of the deficiency in his lot or tract of land

3rd. I give and bequeath to my Grandson Joseph P. Howard son of my won William Howard two hundred dollars which may be P -256 paid to him when he becomes twenty one years of age in two horses bridle and saddle on account of the deficiency in his fathers tract or lot of land

And then after all my Just debts are paid off and the above legatees are paid off, my will and desire is that the balance of my estate, whatever there is may be equally devided between my son James Howard and his his heirs my son J. P. Howard and his heirs my grandson Joseph William Howard to be paid to him at twenty one years of age and my two grandsons William H. Conn and Richard G. Conn

I appoint my brother John Bryant Sr. and my son John P. Howard executors of this my last will and testament and I do revoke all wills by me heretofore made and do by these presents acknowledge this to be my last will and testament. Signed sealed acknowledged this 30th day of December A. D. 1853 in the year of our Lord one Thousand eight hundred and fifty three

Sarah Howard (SEAL)

Signed sealed and acknowledged in our presence
Attest
W. M. Austell
John P Hindman

P-257 State of Tennessee
Coffee County

At a County Court began and held for Coffee County at the Court house in the town of Manchester on the 4th day of December 1854 being the first Monday in said month the foregoing last will and testament of Sarah Howard deceased was produced in Court and proven by the oaths of W. M. Austell and John P. Hindman the subscribing witnesses thereto and ordered to be recorded which is accordingly done this 13th day of December 1854 Hiram S Emerson Clerk

I, JOHN A. JACOBS do this day make and publish this my last will and testament hereby revoking and making void all other wills by me at any time made

1st. I direct that my funeral expenses and all my just debts be paid out of the first money that may come into the hands of my executors

2nd. I direct that all my property shall be sold and that after my debts and expenses are paid the remainder shall go to Joseph A. Sherrill for to be appropriated for his education and I direct that the same shall remain in the hands of my executor to be used for that purpose

3rd. I do hereby nominate and appoint E. H. White my executor and wish the Court at the expiration of his term to appoint him guardian for the above named Joseph A Sherrill

In witness whereof I do hereunto set my hand and seal this
P-258 26th day of February 1856   John A Jacobs (SEAL)
Signed sealed and delivered in our presence the day and date
above written   Richard Messick
                                       Lilburn Butler

State of Tennessee
Coffee County

At a County Court began and held for Coffee County at the Courthouse in the town of Manchester on the 3rd day of March 18 1856 the foregoing will of John A. Jacobs was produced to Court by E. H. White the executor therein named and proven by the oaths of Richard Messick and Lilburn Butler the subscribing witnesses thereto in open Court and ordered to be recorded which is accordingly done

Witness my hand at Office this 5th day of March 1856
                                       Hiram S Emerson Clerk

I, JESSE JENKINS of the County of Coffee and State of Tennessee do make and publish this my last will and testament hereby revoking and making void all other wills by me at any time made

And first I desire that my body be decently buried in a manner suitable to my condition in life and as to such worldly goods as it has pleased God to intrust me with I dispose of in the following manner:

1st. I direct that all my debts and funeral expenses be paid as soon after my death as possible out of any money that
P -259 I may die possessed of or that may first come into the h hands of my executors from any portion of my estate real or personal

2nd. I give and bequeath to my beloved wife Nancy Jenkins fifty acres of land including the mansion house where we now live to be laid of in any way she may wish it to be done and a sufficiency of timber from any portion of my land for its support

I also bequeath my wife two negroes viz Peter and Phebe also all my household and kitchen furniture together with my farming utensils and as much of the stock of different kinds as may be neccessary for her support

All the above property my said wife is to have the whole and sole control of during her natural life or widowhood and then to descend and go to my three sons viz. William G. Benjamin F. and James N. Jenkins and the children of my said three sons that is the legal legitamate heirs of their body the said parents to have the use and benefit of said estate during their natural lives and then to be possessed by their said children

My negro woman Nelly who is advanced in life and one of the mother of the family and has been a faithful servant I leave her under the protection of my said three sons but not to be considered in the capacity of a slave

I also leave to my said wife what ready money I may be possessed of at my death

3rd. I give and gequeath unto my beloved son William G Jenkins my negro boy Sam that is to say he is to have the use and labor of said boy during his natural life and then descend to and be possessed by the legal and legitimate heirs of his body whereas my said son William G. has lived for from me for several years which has put it out of my power to afford him he help to do his labor as I have done for my other two sons, therefore when there shall be a proper calculation and adjustment made of each one of my said three sons have heretofore received of me then whatever balance or lack there may be of making said William G. an equivilant with his other two brothers I direct that it be made up to him out of my said estate for the use of himself and his said heirs

4th. I give and bequeath unto my son Benjamin F my negro boy Henry

5th. I give and bequeath unto my beloved son James N my negro boy George Senr. both the latter boys that is Henry and George to be under the Regulations and Restrictions that Samuel the farmer is under

Lastly I direct that all the balance on residue of my estate both real and personal after my death be equally among my said three sons

If at any time It should be practicable or really neccessary to sell all the lands I may possess at my decease and the land by me given to my said wife after her death I direct that the proceeds of the sale of the said land be appropriated to P-261 the use of the said legal heirs of my said three sons in educating them &C &C

The negroes to be equally devided among my said three sons as may be but none of them to be sold under any circumstances whatever except Jack if it should be advisable or become really neccessary that It should be done from some source or other the proceeds to be applied as above directed if the said Jack has to be sold my earnest wish is that he may be sold into as good hands as possible

If my said negro woman Nelly should become unable to labor she is to be supported from my said estate

In conclusion I repeat and again say that this my last

will and testament is to extend to my three sons above named and
their heirs the legitemate and legal issue of their bodies

I do hereby make ordain and appoint my beloved three sons
viz. William G. Jenkins Benjamin F. Jenkins and James N. Jenkins
or any two of them executors to this my last will and testament

In witness whereof I the said Testament have hereunto set
my hand and seal this 26th day of July in the year of our Lord
one thousand eight hundred and forty five. Jesse Jenkins(SEAT.)
Signed sealed and published in the presence of us who have subscribed our names in the presence of the testator and in the
presence of each other   Witnesses   Benj. F. Hollins
                                             Lawson Wileman
                                             Peter S. Holmes
Since writing the within which was my last will and testament
P-262 the negro girl therein by me bequeathed to my beloved
wife Nancy Jenkins has died which makes it neccessary for the
benefit of my said wife to so far alter the within will that
instead of Peter and Phebe as bequeathed to her in the said
last will. I bequeathand give to her a choice of any three negroes that I may die possessed of to her and belong to her
during her natural life and terer to go and be possessed a s
directed in said last will and testament

Also to have the use of and benefit of my farm or as much
as may be neccessary for her support during said time say one
hundred acres including the mansion House

In witness whereof I hereunto set my hand and seal Decer
10th 1847   Jesse Jenkins (SEAL)

     State of Tennessee
Coffee County
     At a County Court began and held for Coffee County at the
Courthouse in the town of Manchester in the 7th day of April
1856 the foregoing last will and testament of Jesse Jenkins
deceased was produced to Court and proven by the oaths of Benj.
F. Hollins and Lawson Wileman two of the subscriving witnesses
thereto and ordered to be recorded which is accordingly done
          Witness my hand at Office this 15th day of April 1856
                              Hiram S. Emerson Clerk

P-263 I, MARTHA WALL do make and publish this my last will and
testament being weak in body but of sound mind After bequeath-
ing my body to the earth from whence it came and my soul to God
who gave it, and after all my just debts are paid I then bequeath as follows

     2nd. I give and bequeath unto my beloved daughter Melvina
P. Allen one dollar

     3rd. I give and bequeath unto my son William P Wall one
full and equal share

     4th. I also give and bequeath unto my son Alexander Wall
one dollar

     5th. I also give and bequeath to my daughter Sarah F.

Green one full and equal share

6th. I give and bequeath to my daughter F. Felkner one dollar

7th. I also give and bequeath unto my daughter Elizabeth A Stroud one dollar

8th. I give and bequeath unto my daughter Emily H. Howard one full and equal share

9th. I also give and bequeath unto Mary Ann one equal and full share

10th. I also give and bequeath unto my son J. W. Wall one dollar

11th. I also give and bequeath unto my daughter Susan Burks one dollar

12th. I also give and bequeath to my son Beverly E Wall one full and equal share of my estate

And Lastly if my lands and household is not sold in my life time at my death my will is that the said land and property be sold and the proceeds thereof be applied as required in the abo above will and testament

Given under my hand and seal as my last will and testament this 15th day of January 1856   Martha Wall (SEAL)
Given in the presence of us witnesses   Henry B. Coffey
                                         John Hawkins

State of Tennessee
Coffee County

At a Count Court began and held for Coffee County at the Court house in the town of Manchester on the 5th day of May 1856 the foregoing last will and testament of Martha Wall was produced to Court and proven by the oaths of John Hawkins one of the subscribing witnesses thereto and ordered to be recorded which is accordingly done

Witness my hand at Office this 26th day of May 1856
                                Hiram S. Emerson Clerk

I, JAMES SHEED of the County of Coffee and State of Tennessee being in sound mind and disposing memory do hereby make and publish this my last will and testament hereby revoking and making void all other wills by me at any time made

And first I direct that my body be decently intered in a manner suitable to my condition in life as to such worldly Estate as it has pleased God to bless me with I dispose of the same in the following manner

1st. I direct that my funeral expenses be paid as soon after my death as possible out of any money that I may die possessed of or that may first come into the hands of my executors from any portion of my estate real or personal

2nd. I give and bequeath unto my beloved wife Sibbil Sheed fifty acres of land including the mansion house and all the out houses and timber from any other part of my land for its support convenient

I also give and bequeath unto my said wife the following negroes to be my wifes during her natural life or widowhood Becca Millia Suk and Sarah and then to descend to and be equally devided among my four sons (viz) William R Sheed Jesse J Sheed James M Shed and Henry S. Sheed

The above named land and improvements to be possessed by my said son Henry S all the balance of which lands I now possess at my decease and also to possess the above fifty acres at the decease of my wife and he the said Henry S Shed to pay his brother Jesse J. Sheed five hundred dollars

I give and bequeath unto the children of my daughter Nancy M Carl deceased, that is Elizabeth A, James H, William Manson, Bartly B, Thomas B, Jesse J, one hundred dollars each to be paid out of my said estate as early as possible after they come of age

All the balance and residue of my estate I direct to be equally divided among the above named four sons and for them to have the use and benefit of the same during their natural lives and at their decease to go to and be possessed by their natural and legal heirs of their bodies

It is also to be understood that I direct the land bequeathed to my son Henry S Sheed to be by him possessed during h his natural life then to descend to the natural and legal heirs of his body

I do hereby make and appoint my beloved sons Jesse J. Sheed and James M Sheed executors of this my last will and testament

In witness whereof I James Sheed the said testator have hereunto set my hand and seal this 19th day of January in the year of our Lord one thousand and eight hundred and fifty three

James Sheed (SEAL)

Signed Sealed and published in presence of the Testator
Attest   John P. Walker J. F. L. Farris

State of Tennessee
Coffee County

At a County Court began and held for Coffee County at the Court house in the town of Manchester on the 2nd day of June 1856 the foregoing last will and testament of James Sheed deceased was produced to Court and proven by the oath of J. F. L. Farris one of the subscribing witnesses thereto and ordered to be recorded the other subscribing witness having removed from this State and the same is accordingly truly recorded

P-267

Witness Hiram S Emerson Clerk of said Court at Office this 4th day of June 1856   Hiram S. Emerson

I, ELIAS TEAL do make and publish this my last will and testament hereby revoking and making void all other wills by me at any time made

1st. It is my desire that my funeral expenses and all my just debts be paid as soon after my death as possible out of any money that I may die possessed of or that may first come in to the hands of my executors

2nd. I give and bequeath to my two children Langton and Nancy Ann all my real and personal property to be equally devided between them share and share alike when the youngest shall become of age

3rd. Should both of my children die before they become of age leaving no heirs of their body I then desire and is my will that all my slaves to wit Sarah Bill Jo Jane Peter Tony Clenton Fannie Martha Mary Mariah Rebecca Betsy and Hecctor be set free and sent to Libera on the Coast of Africa and that all my property real and personal be sold and the proceeds thereof be used by my executors to remove said slaves as above named and that th the balance of the funds over and above defraying their expenses be equally distributed among them by my said executors share and share alike

4th. I give and bequeath one acre of land including the graves of my father and mother be laid of_ by my said executors for a burying grounds and should I die before I have it done, It is my desire that my executors build a substantial rock wall around said graves so as to include my sisters graves and large enough for myself and children

I also give and bequeath for a Babtist church all that portion of a tract of land I bought of the Bell estate lying south of the Murfreesboro and Manchester Road

I do nominate and appoint W. R. McFadin of the County of Rutherford guardian of my said children and desire him when they become old enough to start to school and sooner if neccessary to take them and raise them and attend to their education

Also should my executors think proper they may let my slave Martha attend them to wait on them

And Lastly I do hereby nominate and appoint W R McFadin and and A. Maxwell my executors and it is my will that all my property except what personal property not included in the article between Robert Teal and myself and the property which came by my last wife be kept together until my children become of age P-269 and that my executors have power to employ some suitable person to carry on my farm And if after Robert Teal present engagement expires and he wishes it and they can agree upon terms I desire he shall continue at least until my son Langston becomes old enough to manage the farm and then if my executors think it would be proper I desire him to be employed I also wish my slaves well fed and clothed and suitably attended in sickness should my children die before they become of age I want my executors to give the two beds and furniture that came by my last wife to her sisters

In witness whereof I do to this my will set my hand and seal this March 6th 1856   Elias Teal   (SEAL)
Signed sealed and published in our presence and we have set our names hereto in the presence of the testator this March 6th 1856
Witness   James A Brantley

At the request of Elias Teal I assign my name as a Witness to
this will this September loth 1856   L. Barnum
                         Codicil
As the partnership that existed between Robert Teal and my self
when I made my will as above has been broken or disolved by mut-
ual consent, it is now my desire that my said will be changed in
the following particulars to wit:
        I desire now that instead of keeping up the farm my execu-
tors shall hire out all the negroes except the one to go with
the children and rent out the farm annually or for a longer
P-270 term of years in their discretion
        It is also my express will that my executors shall not
rent the farm or hire any of the negroes to any of my relatives
        In witness whereof I do set my name to this codicil to my
will this September 10th 1856   Elias Teal (SEAL)
Signed Sealed and published in our presence and we have set our
names hereto in the presence of the testator Sept 10th 1856
Witnesses   J. A. Brantly
                                       L. Barnum

State of Tennessee
Coffee County
        At a County Cpurt began and held for Coffee County at the
Court house in the town of Manchester on the 1st day of Decem-
ber1856 the foregoing last will and testament of Elias Teal deceased was produced to Court and proven by the oaths of James
A Brantly and L Burnam the subscribing witnesses thereto and
ordered to be recorded which is accordingly done
        Witness my hand at Office this 5th day of December 1856
                                Hiram S. Emerson Clerk

        On the 24th day of November 1856 MARY CARNEY Wife of Jos-
eph Carney deceased and of the State of Tennessee and County
of Coffee in her last sickness living with Smith Carney died
on the above day called her Grandson Smith unto her while she
was lying in bed and told her Grandson Smith Carney to settle
with Legsand who is her Grandson also the said Legsand Carney
for the hire of a negro man by the name of Monday and the said
Smith Carney asked her his grandmother Mary Carney did she
want him to have that money and she said she wanted Smith Carney to have it all she died on the next day being the 25th day
of November 1856 Tuesday morning the conversation above spoken
of took place on Monday the day following her death.
                              Rhoda (X) Coffett (SEAL)
                              Delila (X) Watson (SEAL)
Sworn and subscribed before me this 2nd day of March 1857
                              Hiram S Emerson Clk

State of Tennessee
Coffee County

At a County Court began and held for Coffee County at the Court house in the town of Manchester on the 2nd day of March 1857 the foregoing Nuncupative will of Mary Carney was produced to Court and proven by the oaths of Rhoda Coffutt and Delila Watson and ordered to be recorded which is accordingly done

Witness my hand at Office this 4th day of March 1857

Hiram S Emerson Clerk

The Nuncupative will of WILLIAM FARRIS deceased late of the County of Coffee and State of Tennessee made at the Residence P-272 of J. F. L. Farris in said County with whom the decedant was living at the time of her death

Agreeable to statements made by him during his last sickness about one week before his death which death was the 24th of August 1856 to wit:

That it was his will and wish that a note for one hundred dollars on Samuel Russell due the 25th day of December 1857 should be delivered to James R. Farris Jr a grandson of said decedant and that we J. F. L. Farris, Arrona Farris were called upon to bear witness that it was his will that the above mentioned note should go to his Grandson James R. Farris Jr which was at the house affiants during the last sickness of of the said William Farris and Affiants believe he possessed at the time a sound disposing mind and memory

Witness our hands this 1st day of September 1856

J. F. L. Farris
Arrona Farris

Sworn to and subscribed to in open Court this 1st day of September 1856

State of Tennessee
Coffee County

At a County Court began and held for Coffee County at the Court house in the town of Manchester on the 5th day of May 1857 the foregoing Nuncapative will of William Farris deceased was proven by the oaths of J. F. L. Farris and ordered to be recorded which is accordingly done this 7th May 1857

Hiram S. Emerson Clerk

I, JAMES STEPHENS, being of sound mind and disposing memory but feeble in body doth make and publish this my last will and testament to wit

1st, I desire that my funeral expenses and all my Just debts be paid out of any money or means that I might die seized and possessed of and as soon as practicable

2nd. To my beloved wife Belinda Stephens I give and bequeath all my personality of all kinds whatever as well as all my realestate during her natural life to enable her to raise and educate my children not however in anywise to interfere with the possession I have my son William B. to hold so long as he may choose to live on it say the thirty acre tract

3rd. After the death of my said wife It is my will that
the remainder of the property be equally devided among my
heirs if a devision can be made including the Real Estate but
if a devision cannot be made without prejudice to the some of
the heirs then I desire a sale and the proceeds to be equally
devided

4th. Having asked and obtained the consent of Willis Blanton to become the executor to this my will I do therefore constitute him as my executor to carry out my will as set out
above

Given under my hand and seal this 25th day of May 1857

James Stephens (SEAL)

Attests   F. J. Kennady

J. B. Smith

State of Tennessee
Coffee County
P-274 At a County Court began and held for Coffee County at the
Court house in the town of Manchester on the 6th day of July
1857 the foregoing last will and testament of James Stephens
deceased was produced to Court and proven by the oath of F. J.
Kennady one of the subscribing witnesses thereto and ordered to
be recorded which is accordingly done

Witness my hand at Office this 13th day of July 1857

Hiram S. Emerson Clerk

I, FRANKLIN SUGG of the County of Coffee and State of Tennessee Planter do make and publish this my last will and testament hereby revoking and making void all other wills by me at
any time heretofore made

And first I direct that my body be decently intered at the
grave yard at home by the side of Brother Elijah Sugg in said
County in a manner suitable to my condition in life and as to
such worldly estate as it has pleased God to intrust me with I
dispose of the same as follows

1st. I direct that all my debts and funeral expenses be
paid as soon after my death as possible out of any money that
I may die possessed of or that may first come into the hands of
my executors from any portion of my setate real or personal

2nd. I give and bequeath to my sister Lewena Sugg a certain tract of piece of land containing about seventy five acres
and also to my sister Lewena Sugg my interest in a tract of land
P-275 willed to me and Lewena Sugg by Elijah Sugg deceased

3rd. I give and bequeath to my sister Lewena Sugg for her
kindness to me in my affliction and to father &C. all my horses
and interest in horses on the farm and all my hogs and sheep
and all my cattle and one large yoke of oxen and wagon and mans
saddle and bridle and one other saddle of Eligah Sugg

4th. I give and bequeath to my sister Lewena Sugg all my
kitchen and household furniture and also my library of books
and also a set of Black Smith tools and all my farming utensils
&C

5th. I desire that my father Hubbert Sugg be supported during h
his lifetime off of the farm and stock. that his funeral expenses be paid out of the same

6th. I will and bequeath to my sister Lewena Sugg four
shares two in my own name and two in the name of Elijah in the
McMinnville and Manchester Rail Road and also my rail road cer-
tificates these in my name and these in the name of Elijah Sugg
and also two notes one for five dollars and one for six dollars

I do hereby make ordain and appoint my esteemed neighbor
and friend F. M. Yell esquire and beloved sister Lewena Sugg
executors of this my last will and testament

In witness whereof I Franklin Sugg the said testemor have
to this my will written on one sheet of paper set my hand and
seal this 18th day of May one thousand eight hundred and fifty
seven   Franklin Sugg (SEAL)
P-276 Interterred before signed sealed and published in the presence of the testator and of each other
Witnesses   H. W. Carrol
                                    Joseph S Gray
                                    John Anthony

State of Tennessee
Coffee County

At a County Court began and held for Coffee County at the
Court house in the town of Manchester on the 3rd day of August
1857 the foregoing last will and testament of Franklin Sugg deceased was produced to Court by F. M. Yell Exer. and Lewena Sugg
Executrix therein named and proven by the oaths of H. W. Carroll
Joseph S Gray and John Anthony the subscribing witnesses thereto
and ordered to be recorded which is accordingly done

Witness my hand at Office this 10th day of August 1857
                                    Hiram S. Emerson Clerk

I, RUTHA MILLER do make and publish this my last will and
testament hereby revoking and making void all other wills by me
at any time made

1st. I direct that all my funeral expenses and all my debts
be paid as soon after my death as possible out of any money
that I may die possessed of or that may first come into the
hands of my executors

2nd. I give and bequeath to my daughter M. A. Call to have
to her sole and seperate use all of my money and property of
every kind after all my just debts are paid to have during her
natural life and then to her bodily heirs

I do hereby nominate and appoint James M. Call my executor
to this my last will and testament.

In witness whereof I do to this my will set my hand and
seal this 7th day of February in the year of our Lord one thousand eight hundred and fifty seven   Rutha (X) Miller
Attest   Wm. H. Harris
                                      S. W. Chapman

State of Tennessee
Coffee County
        At a County Court began and held for Coffee County at the
Court house in the town of Manchester on the 3rd day of August
1857 the foregoing last will and testament of Rutha Miller deceased was produced to Court by James H. Call the executor
therein named and proven by the oaths of Wm. H. Harris and G.W.
Chapman the subscribing witnesses thereto and ordered to be recorded which is accordingly done
        Witness my hand at Office this 10th day of August 1857
                                            Hiram S Emerson Clerk

P-278   HULDAH MASON do make and publish this my last will and
testament hereby revoking all other wills by me at any time made
        1st. I desire my funeral expenses and just debts paid as
soon as practicable after my death
        2nd. I give to my brother Asa Thomas my negro woman Caro-
line and her four children Cynna Moss Mary & Martha during his
natural life and at his death the same to go to his children
living at his death but he is to permit the girl Cynna to live
with Mrs Stephens wife of Elmathen Stephens so long as Mrs
Stephens resides in Middle Tennessee upon her death or removal
from Middle Tennessee said girl to be delivered to said Asa
Thomas for life as above stated
        3rd. My negro man Drew I desire to be set free but as I
cannot do that I will him to my brother Aso Thomas who I know
will take care of him as he is now old and as he has been a
faithful servant I desire him well cared for and he may become
a charge upon my said brother I give him one hundred dollars to
enable him to take care of him
        4th. My other negroes Ben and Tena and Tenas child as well
as all money on hand notes and accounts due me after the payment of my debts and funeral expenses as wellas all my stock and
farming utensils. I direct to be equally devided among my brothers share and share alike except Aso Thomas who is not to have
any portion further than as above provided for him
        The stock &C will have to be sold in order to devide the
proceeds but the negroes I do not want sold if they can justly
be devided
P-279 My household and kitchen furniture waring apparel &C I
give to my sisters to be equally devided between them
        6th. I hereby nominate and appoint my brother Aso Thomas
executor of this my last will and testament October 4th 1856
                                            Huldah Mason (SEAL)
        Attest   W. P. Hickerson
                                            William McMichael

State of Tennessee
Coffee County
        At a County Court began and held for Coffee County at the
Court house in the town of Manchester on the 2nd day of Novem-

ber 1857 the foregoing last will and testament of Huldah Mason was produced to the Court and proven by the oaths of W. P. Hickerson and William McMichael the subscribing witnesses thereto and ordered to be recorded which is accordingly done

Witness my hand at Office this 5th day of November 1857

Hiram S. Emerson Clerk

October 31st 1857

I, LEANDER HICKERSON do make and publish this my last will and testament hereby revoking and making void all other wills by me at any time made

1st. I direct my soul to God who gave it

2nd. I direct that my funeral expenses and all my just debts be paid as soon after my death as possible out of any money that I may die possessed of or that may first come into the hands of my executors

3rd. I want the Grave Yard where my father and mother are laid and where I want to be laid filled in with cast palings sufficiently large for all my brothers and sisters that my wish to be laid there

I also give one acres of ground around said graves including the old grave yard and a way to get to the same that is not to be obstructed

4th. I will to Leander Vance Hickerson and Leander Hickerson Hord each five hundred dollars which is to be put out at interest until they become of age

5th. I will unto Gabriel Maupin and Sarah His wife one dollar for their unkindness to me

6th. I will and bequeath to William A. Hickerson Wiley Hickerson David Hickerson Litle Hickerson Joseph Hickerson John Hickerson Washington Hickerson and Adelaide Hord all my property personal and Real shall be equally devided among the above named brothers and sister

Lastly I do hereby nominate and appoint Wiley Hickerson my executor

In witness whereof I do to this my last will set my hand and seal date above written   Leander Hickerson (SEAL)

Signed and sealed in the presence of us   C. M. Davidson

William McFarland

P-281 State of Tennessee
Coffee County

At a County Court began and held for Coffee County at the Court house in the town of Manchester on the 7th day of December 1857 the foregoing last will and testament of Leanda Hickerson was produced to Court by Wiley Hickerson the executor therein named and proven by the oaths of C M Davidson and William McFarland the subscribing withesses thereto and ordered to be recorded which is accordingly done

Witness Hiram S. Emerson Clerk of our said Court at office this 10th day of December 1857   Hiram S Emerson Clerk

I, GEORGE WAIT doth make and publish this my last will and testament revoking all others.

After leaving my spirit in the hands of the Almighty God who gave it I wish my property disposed of in the following manner

1st. To pay my funeral expenses and all my just debts after that I wish what is left to devide by sale or otherwise to my daughters Lydia M Elizabeth P. Ann B Beccky and Warren Wait equally between my first named five children and their representatives if she should die first and it is further my will that If I should obtain other property by purchase or otherwise here after that the same shall go to my first named five children P-282 equally or their representatives be said property real or personal and further if I should intermarry with any woman and she should bear child or children they are to share equally with the above five and If I should leave a widow I wish my executor to amply provide a life support for her

I hereby authorize my executor to sell lands as well as personal property and make title to the same for the purpose above named

I hereby appoint Warren Waite my executor to this my will and hereby request the Court not to ask any security of him as such but grant him full power to execute the above will without security

Given under my hand and seal this 13th day of April 1857

George Waite (SEAL)

State of Tennessee
Coffee County

At a County Court began and held for Coffee County at the Court house in the town of Manchester on the 4th day of January 1858 the foregoing last will and testament of George Waite deceased was produced to Court by Warren Waite the executor therein named whereupon W. P. Hickerson Hiram S. Emerson C. C. Brewer and William A. Hickerson was introduced as Witnesses who being duly sworn stated that they were acquainted with the handwriting of said George Waite and thatthey believe the will offered before the Court is in the handwriting of said George Waite deceased wholey and there being no subscribing witnesses P-283 to said will, it is ordered that the same be admitted to Record which is accordingly done.

Witness my hand at Office this 8th day of January 1858

Hiram S. Emerson Clerk

I, RICHARD BLANTON of the County of Coffee and State of Tennessee, Planter, do make and publish this my last will and testament hereby revoking and making void all other wills by me at any time made.

And first I direct that my body be decently intered at the grave at the Old Remancs of John Campbell deceased in said County in a manner suitable to my condition in life, and as to

such worldly estate as it hath pleased God to intrust me with I
dispose of the same as follows.

    1st. I direct that all my just debts and funeral expenses
be paid as soon after my decease as possible out of any money I
may die possessed of or that may first come into the hand of my
executors from any portion of my estate Real or Personal

    2nd. I give and bequeath to my wife Sarah L. Blanton Thomas
T. Blanton Susan E Blanton John A. Blanton Felio E Blanton and
Richard D. Blanton a certain tract of parcel of land wherein I
now live containing about one hundred and thirty acres, when
the youngest child come of age.

    If they all think best to sell the land and devide the same
equally between them all.
P-284 3rd. I give and bequeath to my Sarah the land above bequeathed untill the youngest child comes of age for a home to
live on and raise and educate her children

    4th. I give and bequeath to my wife Sarah Blanton all my
horses hogs cattle & sheep and also the household and kitchen
furniture to help raise the family &C. And monies what are or w
will be due me and also my farming utensils &C.

    I do hereby nominate make and appoint my beloved wife Sa-
rah Blanton and my brother Coleman Blanton executors of this
my last will and testament

    And also I advise the Honorable Court to not bind them to
give bond and security &C.

    In witness whereof I Richard Blanton the said testator
have to this my will written on one sheet of paper set my hand
and seal this 9th day of May A. D. 1858. Richard Blanton (SEAL)
Signed Sealed and published in the presence of the testator and
of each other   Patton Gonases
                                    F. M. Yell

State of Tennessee
Coffee County

    At a County Court began and held for Coffee County at the
Court house in the town of Manchester on the 6th day of September 1858 the foregoing last will and testament of Richard Blanton deceased was produced to Court and proven by the oath of F.
M. Yell one of the subscribing witnesses thereto and ordered to
be recorded which is accordingly done
P-285 Witness my hand at Office this 21st day of September 1858
                                    Hiram S Emerson Clerk

                In the name of God Amen
    I, CHARLES TIMMONS of the County of Lincoln and State of
Tennessee being of sound mind and perfect recollections make
this my last will and testament

    1st. I bequeath my soul unto God who gave it.

    2nd. That all my just debts shall be paid

    3rd. I give and bequeath unto my beloved wife Amy all of
my real and personal estate during her natural life and after

her death I give and bequeath unto my two children all the property both personal and real to be devided among them as follows to wit,

I give to Alexander and James my two youngest sons all of my lands to be equally devided between them, and as I have given to my children Priscella, Ambrose Thomas and Virginia M. heretofore four hundred dollars each I give unto my two daughters Malinda and Susan the like sum of four hundred to make them equal with Priscella, Ambrose Thomas and Virginia M and if my two daughters Malinda and Susan or either of them should receive any of or all of the said four hundred dollars before my beloved wife's death such amount so removed shall be kept an account of.

P-286 I further will that my two grandchildren Charles and William Tuch shall have each a horse and saddle of the Value of Eighty dollars and that Mattory Tuck the mother of Charles and William Tuck have two hundred dollars

And further that Alexander and James support and Comfortly clothe my son William during his life or if he William should marry and have an heir or heirs, then said Alexander and James shall relinquish one fourth of the land to Williams heirs and the devide the balance equally between them and I further will that my daughter Mattory and her two children Charles and William Tuck be supported off of the farm and have part of the house during her widowhood or until her two sons become of age

I further will that my negroes and perishable property be sold and the proceeds equally devided between my son Ambrose Priscella Hodge Thomas Virginia M. Lindey Matory Tuck Malinda and Susan providen that Malinda and Susan have received their four hundred dollars each, Matery her two hundred dollars before an equal devision in made

I further will that if my beloved wife Amy die before my youngest son James becomes of age the property not be sold until he James is twenty one years old

I further will that if Charles and William Tuck are put to a trade that my sons Alexander and James shall not support them further as long as they stay on the farm they Charles and P-287 William Tuck they are to labor while not at school

Charles Timmons (SEAL)

Signed in our presence James A Chitcock, Alfred Smith

State of Tennessee
Coffee County

At a County Court began and held for Coffee County at the Court house in the town of Manchester on the 7th day of February 1859 the foregoing will and testament of Charles Timmons deceased was produced to Court and proven by the oath of James R Chitcock one of the Subscribing witnesses thereto and ordered to be recorded which is accordingly done

Witness my hand at Office this 14th day of February 1859

Hiram S Emerson Clerk

I. SAMUEL BOYD do make and publish this my last will and te
testament hereby revoking and making void all other wills by me
at any time made

    1st. I direct that my funeral expenses and all my debts be
paid as soon as possible out of any money that I may die possessed of or that may first come into the hands of my executors

    2nd. I give and bequeath unto my beloved wife Dorcas Eliza
Boyd the tract of land upon which I now live containing one hundred and thirty three acres more or less and the hereditiments
thereto belonging during her natural life but should it become
P-288 neccessary at any time to sell the land, she has full power to do so and make tittle to the same collect the proceeds or
dispose of the same for the use and benefit of her children and
self and at her death the remainder if any to be devided equally
between my children.

    Lastly I do hereby nominate and appoint my wife Dorcas
Eliza Boyd my executrix

    I witness whereof I do to this my will set my hand and seal
this 1st day of October 1858   Samuel Boyd (SEAL)
Signed sealed and published in our presence and we have subscribed our names hereto in the presence of the testator this first
day of October 1858 Witnesses   B. F. Jenkins
                                    B. H. Wood

State of Tennessee
Coffee County

    At a County Court began and held for Coffee County at the
Court house in the town of Mancheester on the 7th day of Februa-
ary 1859 the foregoing last will and testament of William Boyd
was produced to Court and proven by the oath of B. F. Jenkins
and B. H. Woods the subscribing witnesses thereto and ordered to
be recorded which is accordingly done

    Witness my hand at Office this 14th day of February 1859
                              Hiram S Emesson Clerk

P-289   In the name of God Amen
I, AMBROSE TIMMONS do make and puglish this my last will and
testament hereby revomking all other wills by me at any time
made

    1st. I give my soul to God who gave it.

    2nd. I desire all my Just debts to be paid as well as my
funeral expenses, out of any money that may come into the hands
of my executors hereinafter named

    3rd. I will and bequeath to my beloved wife Lucy Timmons
all my property of every discription including real and personal
estate to have and to hold during her natural life with power
in her to sell such of my personal property as she can best
spare, sufficient to pay off my Just debts.

    4th. At the death of my said wife I direct that all the
property be equally devided between all my children, except my
unfortunate little daughter Effie who is blind she is to have a

choice negro to be selected by her at her mothers death over and above an equal share with the other children

My two grand children William and Ambrose Blackburn children of my deceased daughter Nancy Ann are to have the same portion that the mother would have been entitled to.

I advanced to their mother two hundred dollars which they are to account for in receiving their portion of the estate.

Any advancement I or my wife may make to any of the children is to be charged to such children in the same way.
P-290

5th. Should my wife live untill the youngest child James comes of age, I then recommend that my daughter Effie live with him, but in any wnat I recommend the helpless child to the kindness and care of all my children and charge them to be kind to her helpless and dependent condition.

6th. My wife has power during her natural life to make such advancements to the children or any of them as she deems they may need and be likely to take care of.

7th. I hereby nominate and appoint my wife Lucy Timmons executrix of this my last will and testament

Ambrose Timmons (SEAL)

Signed and Sealed by the testator in our presence and by us subscribed in the presence ot the testator September 29th 1856
Attest
W. P. Hickerson
J. W. Frazier

State of Tennessee
Coffee County

At a County Court betan and held for Coffee County at the Court house in the town of Manchester on the 6th day of December 1858 the fortgoing last will and testament of Ambrose Timmons deceased was produced to Court and proven by the oathe of W. P. Hickerson and J. W. Frazier the subscribing
P -291
witnesses thereto and ordered to be recorded which is accordingly done

Witness my hand at Office this 14th day of February 1859
Hiram S Emerson Clerk

ALDRIDGE, Eliza, 171
ALDRIDGE, John, 171
ALLEN, Benjamin, 84
ALLEN, Katie, 118
ALLEN, Melvina P., 263
ALLISON, John, 207
ALLISON, Thomas [page 48 in this bk], 178
ANDERSON, P. B. (Col.), 85
ANDERSON, Thomas [page 48 in this bk], 178
ANTHONY, John, 253
ANTHONY, John, 275
ARMSTRONG, John, 118
ASHLEY, Wm., 238
ATKINSON, Thomas, 222
AUSTELL, W. M., 256
AUSTELL, Wm., 216
AUSTON, Nancy, 113
AVANT, James M., 184
BANKS, John, 201
BANKS, S. [page 48 in this bk], 178
BARNUM, L., 269
BEALS, Jane, 231
BEAN, Leroy D., 91
BEAN, Lucinda, 91
BECKNELL, Elizabeth, 200
BELLIUMS, Rachael, 127
BERRY, Edward, 116
BERRY, John, 117
BERRY, John, 117
BERRY, Josiah, 117
BERRY, Josiah, 117
BERRY, Samuel, 117
BERRY, Sanford, 116
BERRY, Wm., 116
BERRY (SLAVE), Minga (m), 116
BINGHAM, Ann [page 48 in this bk], 178
BINGHAM, Mary [page 48 in this bk], 178
BINGHAM, Samuel [page 48 in this bk], 178
BINGHAM, Wm. G. [page 48 in this bk], 178
BLACKBURN, Ambrose, 289
BLACKBURN, Nancy Ann, 289
BLACKBURN, Wm., 289
BLAIR, A. M., 189
BLAIR, Alexander M., 187
BLAIR, Eleanor, 187
BLAIR, L. B., 189
BLAIR, Thomas, 187
BLAIR, Thomas, 189
BLAIR (SLAVE), Cy (m), 187
BLANTON, Coleman, 284
BLANTON, Felio E., 283
BLANTON, John A., 283
BLANTON, Nancy, 232
BLANTON, Richard, 283
BLANTON, Richard D., 283
BLANTON, Sarah L., 283
BLANTON, Smith, 232
BLANTON, Susan E., 283
BLANTON, Thomas L., 283

BLANTON, Willis, 180
BLANTON, Willis, 232
BLANTON, Willis, 241
BLANTON, Willis, 272
BOWAN, Guileemus L., 204
BOWDEN, Cynthea, 171
BOWDEN, F. W., 204
BOWDEN, Frederick [page 29 in this bk], 143
BOWDEN, G. L. [page 29 in this bk], 143
BOWDEN, Nancy [page 29 in this bk], 143
BOWDEN, Wm. [page 29 in this bk], 143
BOWDEN (SLAVE), Ben [page 29 in this bk], 143
BOWDEN (SLAVE), Daniel, 204
BOWDEN (SLAVE), Daniel [page 29 in this bk], 143
BOWDEN (SLAVE), Louiza [page 29 in this bk], 143
BOWDEN (SLAVE), Priscella [page 29 in this bk], 143
BOWDEN (SLAVE), Prisella, 204
BOYD, Dorcas Eliza, 287
BOYD, Samuel, 287
BRANDON, John, 231
BRANTLEY, J. A., 38
BRANTLEY, J. A., 47
BRANTLEY, J. A., 49
BRANTLEY, J. A., 164
BRANTLEY, James A., 209
BRANTLEY, James A., 220
BRANTLEY, James A., 269
BREWER, Henry, 163
BREWER, John, 163
BRITTON, Pricilla, 138
BRIXEY, John O., 143
BRIXEY, W. L., 191
BRIXEY, W. R., 191
BRIXEY, Walton, 191
BRIXEY, Walton, 222
BROOMFIELD, Margaret, 186
BROWN, Andrew J. [page 28 in this bk], 143
BROWN, Ann, 143
BROWN, Elihue [page 28 in this bk], 143
BROWN, Elizabeth, 143
BROWN, Gilbert [page 28 in this bk], 143
BROWN, Henry [page 48 in this bk], 178
BROWN, Houston, 143
BROWN, Jane, 148
BROWN, John sr. [page 28 in this bk], 143
BROWN, Joseph [page 28 in this bk], 143
BROWN, Mary, 143
BROWN, Pauline, 84
BROWN, Phebe, 162
BROWN, Samuel, 84
BROWN, Susan, 84

BROWN, Thomas A., 129
BROWN, Thomas H., 143
BRYAN, Abner, 34
BRYAN, Abner, 249
BRYAN, Edwin Levander, 205
BRYAN, Emly Jane, 205
BRYANT, John, 180
BRYANT, John sr., 256
BUCANNON, Mary, 219
BURGER, S. N., 35
BURKS, Susan, 263
BURROWS, Beverly, 122
BURROWS, Elizabeth, 122
BURTON, E. Leuiza, 160
BURTON, James, 160
BUTLER, Elizabeth, 147
BUTLER, George C., 148
BUTLER, Jefferson, 148
BUTLER, John R., 148
BUTLER, Lilburn, 148
BUTLER, Lilburn, 258
BUTLER, Thomas, 147
BYROM, John, 225
CAGE, A. D., 37
CAGE, Edward, 37
CALL, James M., 276
CALL, M. A., 276
CAMPBELL, Eliza, 136
CAMPBELL, Ellen, 167
CAMPBELL, Felix, 123
CAMPBELL, Felix, 124
CAMPBELL, John, 124
CAMPBELL, John, 168
CAMPBELL, John, 283
CARDEN, Margaret, 117
CARDEN, Martin A., 234
CARDEN, Reuben, 232
CARDEN, Robert C., 234
CARDEN, Wm. L., 234
CARDEN (SLAVE), Clark, 232
CARDEN (SLAVE), Jerry, 234
CARDEN (SLAVE), Martha, 234
CARDEN (SLAVE), Matilda, 232
CARDEN (SLAVE), Peter, 232
CARL, Bartly B. [page 92 in this bk], 263
CARL, Eliz. A. [page 92 in this bk], 263
CARL, James H. [page 92 in this bk], 263
CARL, Jesse J. [page 92 in this bk], 263
CARL, Nancy M. [page 92 in this bk], 263
CARL, Thomas B. [page 92 in this bk], 263
CARL, Wm. Manson[page 92 in this bk], 263
CARLISLE, Robt., 168
CARNEY, Joseph, 131
CARNEY, Joseph, 270
CARNEY, L. A., 132
CARNEY, Legrand H., 132
CARNEY, Legsand, 270
CARNEY, Mary, 131

CARNEY, Mary, 270
CARNEY, Mary, 270
CARNEY, Noahmah (f), 131
CARNEY, Sanders B., 132
CARNEY, Signard H., 132
CARNEY, Smith, 132
CARNEY, Smith, 270
CARNEY (SLAVE), Cherry (f), 133
CARNEY (SLAVE), Davy, 132
CARNEY (SLAVE), Edy (f), 132
CARNEY (SLAVE), George, 132
CARNEY (SLAVE), Hector, 131
CARNEY (SLAVE), Indy, 131
CARNEY (SLAVE), Josh, 133
CARNEY (SLAVE), Judy, 131
CARNEY (SLAVE), Monday, 131
CARNEY (SLAVE), Nannie, 133
CARNEY (SLAVE), Patty, 132
CARNEY (SLAVE), Patzy, 131
CARNEY (SLAVE), Pegy, 131
CARNEY (SLAVE), Peter, 132
CARNEY (SLAVE), Tom, 132
CARNEY (SLAVE), Tony, 132
CARROL, H. W., 275
CARROLL, A. W., 253
CARROLL, John, 166
CARROLL, Wm., 253
CARTWRIGHT, Salley, 32
CASEY, Wm., 155
CASS, Moses M., 182
CATE, Biddy, 126
CATE, Elizah, 126
CATE, Henry A., 126
CATE, John, 124
CATE, John B., 126
CATE, Polly, 124
CATE, Priscilla, 124
CATE, Sarah Harriet, 124
CATE, Susanna, 124
CAUTHEN, Hugh R., 86
CAUTHRAN, Jane, 120
CAUTHRAN, Martin, 120
CAUTHRAN, Pleasant, 120
CAUTHRAN, Wm. R., 120
CAVERT, Thomas, 168
CHAPMAN, Geo. W., 168
CHAPMAN, S.? W., 276
CHARLES, John, 207
CHITCOCK, James A., 287
CLANCY, Henrietta, 115
CLARK, Anthony, 191
CLAY, Anthony, 191
CLAYBORNE, Martha J., 244
COFFETT, Rhoda, 270
COFFEY, Henry B., 263
COLLINS, Evy, 160
COLLINS, Wm., 114
COLLINS, Wm., 160
COLLINS, Wm., sr., 161
COLYER, Katherine [page 27 in this bk], 140
CONLSON, Charles, 127

KIRKPATRICK, Jno. C., 185
LAIRD, Felisha, 120
LAMB, Louisa, 113
LAMBERT, Elizabeth, 165
LAWRENCE, J. H., 227
LEFEVER, John, 126
LEFEVER, John, 134
LORD, Elizabeth, 214
LORD, Jeramiah B., 215
LORD, Malissa, 214
LORD, Wm., 212
LOWE, Samuel, 135
LOWERY, Wm., 200
LUSK, James G., 200
LUSK, Joseph, 200
LUSK, Salley, 200
LUSK, Wm., 199
LUSK, Wm., 200
LYNN, Andrew, 210
LYNN, Andrew, 212
LYNN, Andrew Jackson, 212
LYNN, Isabell, 212
LYNN, Jackson, 210
LYNN, Jacob, 212
LYNN, James Calvin, 212
LYNN, Louisa Jane, 212
LYNN, Mathilda, 210
LYNN, Matilda, 212
LYNN, Thomas, 210
LYNN, Thomas, 234
LYNN, Thomas H., 212
LYNN, Wm., 212
LYNN, Wm. E., 212
MABRY, Harriot B., 146
MABRY, Hinehia, 146
MABRY, John, 146
MABRY, Martha M., 146
MABRY, Thomas Elliott, 146
MABRY (SLAVE), Ann, 146
MABRY (SLAVE), Critty, 146
MABRY (SLAVE), Daniel, 146
MABRY (SLAVE), Dark, 146
MABRY (SLAVE), Jane, 146
MARBERY, L. W., 246
MARSHALL, Berry, 118
MARSHALL, Fersy? (f), 118
MARSHALL, Henry, 118
MARSHALL, James B., 118
MARSHALL, John, 118
MARSHALL, Margarett, 118
MARSHALL, Nancy, 118
MARSHALL, Wm., 118
MARTIN, Kinchan, 113
MASON, Huldah, 278
MASON, Joseph, 185
MASON, Thomas W., 165
MASON (SLAVE), Ben, 278
MASON (SLAVE), Caroline, 278
MASON (SLAVE), Cynna, 278
MASON (SLAVE), Drew, 278
MASON (SLAVE), Martha, 278
MASON (SLAVE), Mary, 278
MASON (SLAVE), Moss, 278
MASON (SLAVE), Tena (f), 278
MATHEWS, Kinchen, 128
MAUPIN, Gabriel, 279

MAUPIN, Jane B., 236
MAUPIN, Sarah, 279
MAXWELL, A., 38
MAXWELL, A., 46
MAXWELL, A., 189
MAXWELL, A., 209
MAXWELL, A., 229
MAXWELL, A., 267
MAXWELL, Adam, 164
MAXWELL, Andrew, 219
MAYO, James, 124
MCBEE, Samuel, 252
MCBOWDEN, Frederick [page 29 in this bk], 143
MCCLAIN, S., 116
MCCLEAN, Daniel, 143
MCCLEAN, Daniel, 177
MCCLEAN, Danl., 195
MCCRARY, Elizabeth, 124
MCCULLIUGH, Mathilde, 120
MCCULLOUGH, James, 226
MCCULLOUGH, Rhoda, 226
MCCULLOUGH, Rhoda, 226
MCFADIN, W. R., 267
MCFARLAND, Wm., 279
MCGUIRE, Eliza J., 234
MCGUIRE, John B., 162
MCGUIRE, John B., 178
MCGUIRE, Robt., 234
MCLEAN, Daniel, 118
MCMICHAEL, Wm., 279
MESSICK, Catherine, 112
MESSICK, Chrisley, 189
MESSICK, Chrisly, 215
MESSICK, Christy, 112
MESSICK, Crisley, 168
MESSICK, George, 112
MESSICK, Gilbert, 112
MESSICK, Gilbert B., 226
MESSICK, Polly, 112
MESSICK, Richard, 112
MESSICK, Richard, 258
MESSICK, Sally, 112
MILEHAM, Walter, 122
MILLER, George, 244
MILLER, Rutha, 276
MITCHELL, A., 134
MITCHELL, Jobe, 117
MITCHELL, Thomas, 117
MONTGOMERY, Cynthia, 186
MONTGOMERY, David, 185
MONTGOMERY, Easter, 186
MONTGOMERY, Sandyville P., 186
MONTGOMERY, Susan, 186
MOONEY, Wm. S., 122
MOORE, B. F., 47
MOORE, B. F., 220
MOORE, Benjamin, 227
MOORE, Charles, 227
MOORE, Martha, 229
MOORE, Martha A., 229
MOORE, Mary, 227
MOORE, Robert, 227
MOORE, Wm., 227
MOORE (SLAVE), Ann, 227
MOORE (SLAVE), Charles, 227

MOORE (SLAVE), Manuel, 227
MOORE (SLAVE), Mariah, 227
MOORE (SLAVE), Matty, 227
MOORE (SLAVE), Rachael, 227
MORGAN, Angelina, 138
MORGAN, Angelina, 205
MORGAN, Angeline, 206
MORGAN, Ann Amanda, 205
MORGAN, Harwood, 205
MORGAN, Sarah Elizabeth, 205
MORGAN, Wm. Harrison, 205
MORRISON, John F., 121
MORROW, Catharine, 157
MORTON, Langston, 207
MOSS, Matilda, 239
MURRAY, S., 116
MYERS, W. H., 210
NEIL, Alexander, 136
NEIL, Alexander, 167
NEIL, Angelina, 136
NEIL, Angeline, 166
NEIL, Betty, 135
NEIL, Betty, 166
NEIL, Duncan, 166
NEIL, Elizabeth, 136
NEIL, Elizabeth, 167
NEIL, James, 135
NEIL, James, 166
NEIL, Thomas, 136
NEIL, Thomas, 167
NEIL, William, 136
NEIL, Wm., 167
NEIL (SLAVE), John, 136
NEIL (SLAVE), John, 167
NEILE, Duncan, 135
NELSON, D., 231
NELSON, Daniel, 212
NELSON, John, 154
NELSON, Lucy, 154
NELSON, Margaret, 154
NEVILL, Jesse P., 155
NEVILL, Mary, 122
NEVILLE, Mary E., 155
NICHOL, Sarah, 194
NICHOLS, Cynthia, 194
NICHOLS, George, 37
NICHOLS, Jacob, 194
NICHOLS, Levina, 37
NICHOLS, Sarah, 194
NICHOLS, Wm. P., 37
NORTON, Wilson, 133
NORTON, Wm., 203
NORTON, Wm. S., 149
OAKS, Isaac, 129
OAKS, James, 128
OAKS (SLAVE), Jim, 129
OAKS (SLAVE), Lucretia, 129
OAKS (SLAVE), Rose, 129
OLDFIELD, Alexander Neil, 167
OLDFIELD, Charles, 168
OLDFIELD, David, 168
OLDFIELD, Mary, 136
OLDFIELD, Mary, 168
OLDFIELD, Nancy, 136
OLDFIELD, Nancy, 167
ONEIL, John, 212
OSBORNE, G. G., 229

PARKER, Thomas, 148
PARTEN, Hannah, 121
PATTERSON, Abraham, 159
PATTERSON, Elizabeth, 159
PATTERSON, John, 159
PATTERSON, Mary, 159
PATTERSON, Robt., 158
PATTERSON, Susanna, 159
PATTERSON, Thomas, 159
PATTON, Alexander E., 126
PATTON, E. A., 134
PATTON, Joseph J., 168
PEAY, John L., 238
PEAY, Ranny (f), 238
PENDLETON, Edmond, 208
PENN, John, 136
PENN, John, 167
PETTY, Eli, 140
PETTY, Eli, 156
PETTY, Eli, 158
PETTY, R. M.?, 158
PETTY, Robt. M., 156
PHILLIPS, James, 200
PHILLIPS, Johnathan, 198
PHILLIPS, Johnson, 199
PHILLIPS, N. C., 168
PHILLIPS, Ruth, 200
PHILLIPS, Sarah, 198
PHILLIPS, Wm. Y., 198
PHILLIPS (SLAVE), Lewis, 198
POINDEXTER, Amanda J., 187
POWERS, Delphis, 171
POWERS, Effie, 171
POWERS, Henry, 140
POWERS, Henry [page 48 in this bk], 178
POWERS, Thomas, 171
POWERS, Thomas, 183
POWERS, Thomas, 222
PRICE, F. F., 236
PRICE, P. H., 232
PRICE, R. R., 236
QUALLS, John, 113
QUALLS, Martha, 113
QUALLS, Mary, 113
QUALLS, Wm., 113
RALPH, David [page 48 in this bk], 178
RAMSEY, David [page 29 in this bk], 143
RANKINS, Nancy (dec'd), 32
RANKINS, Wm. G., 32
RAYBURN, Adam, 164
RAYBURN, Adam, 208
RAYBURN, James G., 209
RAYBURN, Mary, 164
RAYBURN, Robert S., 163
RAYBURN, Sarah, 209
RAYBURN (SLAVE), Caroline, 209
RAYBURN (SLAVE), Clayburn, 164
READY, Charles, 149
REYNOLDS, Elestra, 207
REYNOLDS, Elisha, 208
RICHARDSON, Giles, 198
ROACH, Charles S., 162